J. KRISHNAMURTI
THE WHOLE MOVEMENT OF LIFE IS LEARNING

Letters to the Schools

For more information please contact
Krishnamurti Foundation Trust Ltd.
Brockwood Park, Bramdean, Hampshire
SO24 0LQ, England.
E-mail: info@kfoundation.org · Website: www.kfoundation.org

J. Krishnamurti

The Whole Movement of Life is Learning

Letters to the Schools

CONTENTS

1. Total Education...13

2. Goodness..15

3. Leisure..17

4. Fear..20

5. Knowledge...23

6. Responsibility..26

7. Learning...30

8. Radical Change..33

9. Diligence..36

10. Security...39

11. Comparison...42

12. Psychological Wounds..45

13. Habit...48

14. Beauty...51

15. Capacity..54

16. Insight And Honesty...57

17. Desire And Disorder...60

18. Integrity..64

19. Problems...68

20. Status..71

21. Sensitivity...74

22. Self-Centredness...77

23. The Art Of Living...80

24. Words..84

25. Intellect...88

26. Violence...91

27. Values..94

28. Centres Of Learning..............................97

29. Human Survival...................................99

30. Cooperation.......................................101

31. Intelligence...104

32. The Movement Of Thought..................106

33. Knowing Yourself...............................109

34. Affection..112

35. Seeing The Fact..................................115

36. Reward And Punishment.....................118

37. Communication..................................121

38. Educating Oneself..............................124

39. Efficiency...126

40. Thinking Together..............................128

41. Attention..130

42. Family And Society.............................132

43. The Vastness Of Life...........................135

44. Awareness..138

45. The Teacher..141

46. Vulnerability......................................144

47. Intention..147

48. Commitment......................................150

49. Vision..153

50. Choice...156

51. The Limitation...................................159

52. Humility..162

53. Mediocrity..165

54. Harmony With Nature...168

55. There Is Only Learning..172

56. Tradition..177

57. Culture..179

58. Obedience..181

59. Conflict...184

60. Working Together..186

61. Order..188

62. Morality..190

63. Action...192

64. Prejudice...194

65. A Different Education..196

66. Fundamental Freedom...199

67. Relationship..202

68. Authority..205

69. Compulsion...207

70. Discipline..210

71. Sanity...214

72. Order And Freedom..218

Editors Note..223

FOREWORD

As I would like to keep in touch with the schools in India, Brockwood Park in England and the Oak Grove School in Ojai, California, I propose to write a letter every fortnight to them for as long as is possible. It is difficult to keep in touch with them all personally, so, if I may, I would very much like to write these letters to convey what the schools should be, to convey to all the people who are responsible for them that these schools are to be excellent academically, but much more. They are to be concerned with the cultivation of the total human being. These centres of education must help the student and the educator to flower naturally. The flowering is really very important; otherwise education becomes merely a mechanical process oriented to a career, to some kind of profession. Career and profession, as society now exists, are inevitable, but if we lay all our emphasis on that, then the freedom to flower will gradually wither. We have laid far too much emphasis on examinations and getting good degrees. That is not the main purpose for which these schools were founded. This does not mean that the student will be inferior academically. On the contrary, with the flowering of the teacher as well as the student, career and profession will take their right place.

These letters are not meant to be read casually when you have a little time from other things, nor are they to be treated as entertainment. These letters are written seriously and if you care to read them, read them with intent to study what is said, as you would study a flower by looking at the flower very carefully – its petals, its stem, its colours, its fragrance and its beauty. These letters should be studied in the same manner, not read one morning and forgotten in the rest of the day. One must give time to it, play with it, question it, inquire into it without acceptance. Live with it for some time; digest it so that it is yours and not the writer's.

J Krishnamurti

1. TOTAL EDUCATION

*These schools are
to cultivate the total human being*

Society, the culture in which we live, demands that the student must be oriented towards a job and physical security. This has been the constant pressure of all societies: career first and everything else second; that is, money first and the complex ways of our daily life second. We are trying to reverse this process, because man cannot be happy with money only. When money becomes the dominant factor in life, there is imbalance in our daily activity. I would like the educators to understand this very seriously and to see its full significance. If the educator understands the importance of this, and in his own life has given it its proper place, then he can help the student, who is compelled by his parents and society to make a career the most important thing. I would like to emphasize this point – to maintain at all times in these schools a way of life that cultivates the total human being.

As most of our education is the acquisition of knowledge, it is making us more and more mechanical; our minds are functioning along narrow grooves, whether it is scientific, philosophical, religious, business or technological knowledge that we are acquiring. Our ways of life, both at home and outside it, and our specializing in a particular career, are making our minds more and more narrow, limited and incomplete. All this leads to a mechanical way of life, a mental standardization, and so gradually the State, even a democratic State, dictates what we should become. Most thoughtful people are naturally aware of this, but unfortunately they seem to accept it and live with it. This has become a danger to freedom.

Freedom is a very complex issue and to understand the complexity of it, the flowering of the mind is necessary. Each person will give a different definition of the flowering of the mind depending on his culture, on his education, experience, religious superstition – that is, on his conditioning. Here we are not dealing with opinion or prejudice, but rather with a non-verbal understanding of the implications and consequences of the flowering of the mind. This flowering is the total unfoldment and cultivation of our minds, our hearts and our physical well-being; that is to have complete harmony in which there is no opposition or contradiction. The flowering of the mind can take place only when there is clear, objective, non-personal perception, when it is not burdened by any imposition upon it. It is not what to think but how to think clearly. For centuries, through propaganda and so on, we have been encouraged in what to think. Most modern education is that, and not the investigation of the whole movement of thought. Flowering implies freedom. A plant requires freedom to grow.

In every letter we will deal with the awakening of the heart, which is not sentimental, romantic or imaginary, but is of goodness which is born out of affection and love; and with the cultivation of the body, the right kind of food, proper exercise, which will bring about deep sensitivity. When the mind, the heart and the body are in complete harmony, then the flowering comes naturally, easily and in excellence. This is our job, our responsibility as educators. Teaching is the greatest profession in life.

2. GOODNESS

Freedom is essential
for the beauty of goodness

Goodness can flower only in freedom. It cannot bloom in the soil of persuasion in any form, nor under compulsion, nor is it the outcome of reward. It does not reveal itself when there is any kind of imitation or conformity, and it cannot exist when there is fear. Goodness shows itself in behaviour, and this behaviour is based on sensitivity. Goodness is expressed in action. The whole movement of thought is not goodness. Thought, which is very complex, must be understood; the very understanding of it awakens thought to its own limitation.

Goodness has no opposite. Most of us consider goodness to be the opposite of the bad or evil and so, throughout history, in any culture, goodness has been considered the other face of that which is brutal. Humanity has always struggled against evil in order to be good; but goodness can never come into being if there is any form of violence or struggle. Goodness shows itself in behaviour and action and in relationship. Generally, our daily behaviour is based on following certain patterns, which are mechanical and therefore superficial, or on very carefully thought-out motives based on reward or punishment. So our behaviour, consciously or unconsciously, is calculated. This is not good behaviour. When one realizes this, not merely intellectually or by putting words together, then good behaviour comes out of negating what it is not.

Good behaviour is in essence the absence of the self, the "me". It shows itself in politeness, in consideration for others, in yielding without losing integrity. Behaviour is extraordinarily important; it is not a casual affair to be slurred over, or a plaything of a sophisticated mind. It comes out of the depth of your being and is part of your daily existence.

Goodness shows itself in action. To act correctly is one of the most difficult things to do. It is very complex and must be examined very closely without impatience or jumping to any conclusion. In our daily lives, action is a continuous movement from the past broken up occasionally with a new set of conclusions. These conclusions then become the past, so one acts according to preconceived ideas or ideals. One is acting always either from accumulated knowledge, which is the past, or for a future ideal, a utopia. We accept such action as normal. Is it? We question it after it has taken place or before doing it, but this questioning is based on previous conclusions or expectations of future reward or punishment – 'If I do this, I will get that'.

We are now questioning the whole accepted idea of action. Action takes place after we have accumulated knowledge or experience; or we act and learn, pleasantly or unpleasantly, from that action, and this learning again becomes the accumulation of knowledge. So both actions are based on knowledge; they are not different. Knowledge is always the past and so our actions are always mechanical.

Is there an action that is not mechanical, that is non-repetitive, non-routine and so without regret? This is really important for us to understand, for where there is freedom and the flowering of goodness, action can never be mechanical. Writing is mechanical; learning a language, driving a car is mechanical; acquiring any kind of technical knowledge and acting according to that is mechanical. In this mechanical activity there may be a break, and in that break a new conclusion may be formed, but that again becomes mechanical. One must bear in mind constantly that freedom is essential for the beauty of goodness. There is a non-mechanical action, but you have to discover it. You cannot be told about it; you cannot be instructed in it; you cannot learn from examples, for then it becomes imitation and conformity. Then you have lost freedom completely and there is no goodness.

3. LEISURE

Only in leisure can the mind learn

Relationship with another human being is one of the most important things in life. Most of us are not very serious in our relationships, for we are concerned with ourselves first and the other person when it is convenient, satisfying, or sensually gratifying. We treat relationship from a distance, as it were, and not as something in which we are totally involved.

We hardly ever show ourselves to another, for we are not fully aware of ourselves, and what we show to another in relationship is either possessive, dominating or subservient. There is the other and me, two separate entities sustaining a lasting division, each one concerned with himself or herself, and so this division is maintained throughout life until death comes. Of course one shows sympathy, affection, general encouragement, but the divisive process goes on. From this arises incompatibility, the assertion of temperaments and desires, and so there is fear and placation. Sexually there may be coming together, but the peculiar, almost static, relationship of the "you" and the "me" is sustained, with quarrels, hurts, jealousies and all the usual travail. All this is generally considered good relationship.

Now, can goodness flower in all this?

Relationship is life; without some kind of relationship one cannot exist. The hermit, the monk, however they may withdraw from the world, carry the world with them. They may deny it, they may suppress it, they may torture themselves, but they still remain in some kind of relation with the world, for they are the result of thousands of years of tradition, superstition and all the knowledge that man has gathered through millennia. So there is no escape from it all.

There is a relationship between the educator and the student. Does the teacher maintain, whether knowingly or unknowingly, a sense of superiority, always standing on a pedestal, making the student feel inferior, the one who has to be taught? Obviously in this there is no relationship. From this arises fear on the part of the student, a sense of pressure and strain, and therefore the student learns, from his youth, this quality of superiority. He is made to feel belittled, and so throughout life he either becomes the aggressor is continuously yielding and subservient.

A school is a place of leisure, where the educator and the one to be educated are both learning. This is the central fact of the school – to learn. We do not mean by leisure having time to oneself, though that is also necessary. It does not mean taking a book and sitting under a tree or in your bedroom, reading casually. It does not mean having a placid state of mind, and it certainly does not mean being idle or using time for daydreaming. Leisure means a mind that is not constantly occupied with something, with a problem, with some enjoyment, with some sensory pleasure. Leisure implies that a mind has infinite time to observe what is happening around oneself and within oneself, to listen, to see clearly. Leisure implies freedom, which is generally translated as doing as one desires, which is what human beings are doing anyway, causing a great deal of mischief, misery and confusion. Leisure is having a quiet mind, with no motive and so no direction. It is only in this state of leisure that the mind can learn, not only science, history, mathematics but also about oneself. And one can learn about oneself in relationship.

Can all this be taught in our schools, or is it something you read about and either memorize or forget? When the teacher and the taught are involved in really understanding the extraordinary importance of relationship, then they are establishing in the school a right relationship among themselves. This is part of education, greater than merely teaching academic subjects.

Relationship requires a great deal of intelligence. It cannot be bought in a book or be taught. It is not the accumulated result of great experience. Knowledge is not intelligence. Intelligence can use knowledge. Knowledge can be clever, bright and utilitarian, but that is not intelligence. Intelligence can use knowledge. Intelligence comes naturally and easily when the whole nature and structure of relationship is seen. That is why it is important to have leisure so that the man or the woman, the teacher or the student can quietly and seriously talk over their relationship, so that their actual reactions, susceptibilities, and barriers are seen, not imagined, not twisted to please each other or suppressed in order to placate the other.

Surely this is the function of a school: to help the student to awaken his intelligence and to learn the great importance of right relationship.

4. FEAR

Goodness cannot flower
in the field of fear

It appears that most people spend a great deal of time discussing mere verbal clarity; they do not seem to grasp the depth and content beyond the word. In trying to search out verbal clarity, they make their minds mechanical, their lives superficial and very often contradictory. In these letters we are concerned not with verbal understanding, but with the daily facts of our lives. This is the central fact of all these letters – not the verbal explanation of the fact but the fact itself. When we are concerned with verbal clarity and so clarity of ideas, our daily life is conceptual and not factual. All the theories, the principles, the ideals are conceptual. Concepts can be dishonest, hypocritical and illusory. One can have any number of concepts or ideals, but those have nothing whatsoever to do with the daily happenings of our life. People are nurtured on ideals; the more fanciful they are, the more they are considered noble; but the understanding of daily events is far more important than ideals. If one's mind is cluttered with concepts, ideals and so on, the fact, the actual happening can never be faced. The concept becomes a block. When all this is very clearly understood – not intellectually or conceptually – the great importance of facing a fact, the actual, the now, becomes the central factor of our education.

Politics is some kind of universal disease based on concepts; and religion is romantic, imaginary emotionalism. When you observe what is actually going on, all this is an indication of conceptual thinking and an avoidance of the daily misery, confusion and sorrow of our life.

Goodness cannot flower in the field of fear. In this field there are many varieties, the immediate fears and the fears of many tomorrows. Fear is not a concept, but the explanations of fear are conceptual and vary from one pundit to another or from one intellectual to another. The explanation is not important; what is important is facing the fact of fear.

In all our schools the educator and those responsible for the students, whether in the classroom, on the playing field or in their rooms, have the responsibility to see that fear in any form does not arise. The educator must not arouse fear in the student. This is not conceptual, because the educator himself understands, not only verbally, that fear in any form cripples the mind, destroys sensitivity, shrinks the senses. Fear is the heavy burden which man has always carried. From this fear arise various forms of superstition – religious, scientific and imaginary. One lives in a make-believe world, and the essence of the conceptual world is born of fear. We said previously that man cannot live without relationship, and this relationship is not only his own private life but, if he is an educator, he has a direct relationship with the student. If there is any kind of fear in this, then the teacher cannot possibly help the student to be free of it. The student comes from a background of fear, of authority, of all kinds of fanciful and actual impressions and pressures. The educator too has his own pressures, fears. He will not be able to bring about understanding of the nature of fear if he has not uncovered the root of his own fears. It is not that he must first be free of his own fears in order to help the student to be free, but rather that in their daily relationship, in conversation, in class, the teacher will point out that he himself is afraid, as the student is too, and so together they can explore the whole nature and structure of fear.

It must be pointed out that this is not a confessional on the part of the teacher. He is just stating a fact without any emotional, personal emphasis. It is like having a conversation between good friends; it requires a certain honesty and humility. Humility is not servility. Humility is not a sense of defeatism; humility knows neither arrogance nor pride. So the teacher has a tremendous responsibility.

Teaching is the greatest of all professions. The teacher is to bring about a new generation in the world, which is a fact, not a concept. You can make a concept of a fact, and so get lost in concepts, but the actual always remains. Facing the actual, the now, and the fear, is the highest function of the educator; not only to bring about academic excellence but also, what is far more important, the psychological freedom of the student and himself.

When the nature of freedom is understood, then you eliminate all competition on the playing field and in the classroom. Is it possible to eliminate academic or ethical comparative evaluation altogether? Is it possible to help the student not to think competitively in the academic field and yet to have excellence in his studies, his actions and his daily life? Please bear in mind that we are concerned with the flowering of goodness, which cannot possibly be where there is any competition. Competition exists when there is comparison, and comparison does not bring about excellence. These schools fundamentally exist to help both the student and the teacher to flower in goodness. This demands excellence in behaviour, in action and in relationship. This is our intent; this is why these schools have come into being; not to turn out mere careerists but to bring about excellence of spirit.

5. KNOWLEDGE

*Accumulation of knowledge
does not lead to intelligence*

Knowledge will not lead to intelligence. We accumulate a great deal of knowledge about many things, but to act intelligently about what one has learnt seems almost impossible. Schools, colleges and universities cultivate knowledge about our behaviour, about the universe, about science and every form of technology, but these centres of education rarely help a human being to live a daily life of excellence. Scholars maintain that human beings can evolve only through vast accumulations of information and knowledge. Humanity has lived through thousands and thousands of wars; has accumulated a great deal of knowledge on how to kill, yet that very knowledge is preventing us from putting an end to all wars. We accept war as a way of life and all the brutalities, violence and killing as the normal course of our life. We know we should not kill another. This knowing is totally unrelated to the fact of killing; knowledge does not prevent our killing animals and destroying the earth. Knowledge cannot function through intelligence, but intelligence can function with knowledge. To know is not to know; the understanding of the fact that knowledge can never solve our human problems is intelligence.

Education in our schools is not only the acquisition of knowledge, but what is far more important the awakening of intelligence, which will then utilize knowledge. It is never the other way round. The awakening of intelligence is our concern in all these schools. The inevitable question then arises as how this intelligence is to be awakened. What is the system, what is the method, what is the practice? This very question implies that one is still functioning in the field of knowledge. The realization that it is a wrong question is the beginning of the awakening of intelligence. Practice, method, system in our daily lives make for routine, repetitive action and so a mechanical mind. The continuous movement of knowledge, however specialized, puts the mind into a groove, into a narrow way of life. To learn to observe and understand this whole structure of knowledge is to begin to awaken intelligence.

Our minds live in tradition. The very meaning of that word – to hand down – denies intelligence. It is easy and comfortable to follow tradition, whether it is political, religious or self-invented tradition. Then one does not have to think about it; one does not question it, it is part of tradition to accept and obey. The older the culture, the more the mind is bound to the past, lives in the past. The breaking down of one tradition will inevitably be followed by the imposition of another. A mind with many centuries of any particular tradition behind it refuses to let the old go until there is another tradition equally gratifying and secure. Tradition in all its various forms, from the religious to the academic, must deny intelligence. Intelligence is infinite. Knowledge, however vast, is finite, like tradition. In our schools the habit-forming mechanism of the mind must be observed. In this observation there is the quickening of intelligence.

It is part of human tradition to accept fear. Both the older and younger generation live with fear. Most are not aware that we live in fear. It is only in a mild form of crisis or a shattering incident that we become aware of this abiding fear. It is there. Some are aware of it, others shy away from it. Tradition says: control fear, run away from it, suppress it, analyse it, act upon it, or accept it. We have lived with fear for millennia and we somehow manage to get along with it. It is the nature of tradition to act upon it or run away from it, or sentimentally to accept it and look to some outside agency to resolve it. Religions spring from this fear, and the politicians' compelling urge for power is born out of this fear. Any form of domination over another is the nature of fear. When a man or a woman possesses another, there is fear in the background, and this fear destroys every form of relationship.

It is the function of the educator to help the student to face this fear, whether it is fear of the parent, of the teacher or of an older student, the fear of being alone or the fear of nature. The central issue in understanding the nature and structure of fear is to face it; to face it not through the screen of words, but to observe the very happening of fear without any movement away from it. The movement away from the fact is to confound the fact. Our tradition, our education, encourages control, acceptance or denial, or very clever rationalization.

As a teacher, can you help the student and yourself to face every problem that arises in life? In learning, there is neither the teacher nor the taught, there is only learning. To learn about the whole movement of fear we must come to it with curiosity, which has its own vitality. Like a child who is very curious, in that curiosity there is intensity. It is the path of tradition to conquer what we do not understand, to beat it down, to trample it – or to worship it. Tradition is knowledge, and the ending of knowledge is the birth of intelligence.

Now, realizing there is neither the teacher nor the taught but only the act of learning on the part of the grown-up and the student, can you, through direct perception of what is happening, learn about this fear? You can if you will allow fear to tell its ancient story. Listen to it attentively, without interference, for it is telling you the history of your own fear. When you so listen, you will discover that the fear is not separate from you. You are that very fear, that very reaction with a word attached to it. The word is not important. The word is knowledge, the tradition; but the actual, the now that is happening, is something totally new; it is the discovery of the newness of your own fear. Facing the fact of fear, without any movement of thought, is the ending of fear. Not any particular fear but the very root of fear is disintegrated in this observation. There is no observer, only observation.

Fear is a very complex business, as ancient as the hills, ancient as humankind, and it has a very extraordinary story to tell. But you must know the art of listening to it, and there is great beauty in that listening. There is only listening and the story does not exist.

6. RESPONSIBILITY

A human being is the whole of mankind

The word responsibility should be understood in all its significance. It comes from to respond, to respond not partially but wholly. The word also implies to refer back, respond to your background, which is to refer back to your conditioning. Responsibility is the action, as it is generally understood, of one's human conditioning. One's culture, the society in which one lives, naturally conditions the mind, whether that culture is native or foreign. From this background one responds, and this response limits our responsibility. If one is born in India, Europe, America or wherever, one's response will be according to religious superstition – all religions are superstitious structures – or nationalism, or scientific theories. These condition one's response, and they are always limited, finite; and so there is always contradiction, conflict and the arising of confusion. This is inevitable and it brings about division between human beings. Division in any form must bring about not only conflict and violence but ultimately war.

If one understands the actual meaning of the word responsible and what goes on in the world today, one sees that responsibility has become irresponsible. In understanding what is irresponsible, we will begin to comprehend what responsibility is. Responsibility is for the whole, as the word implies, not for oneself, not for one's family; not for some concepts or beliefs, but for the whole of mankind.

Our various cultures have emphasized separateness, called individualism, which has resulted in each one doing what he desires or being committed to his own particular little talent, however profitable or useful that talent may be to society. This does not mean what the totalitarians want one to believe, that only the State and the authorities who represent the State are important, not human beings. The State is a concept, but a human being, though he lives in the State, is not a concept. Fear is an actuality, not a concept.

A human being psychologically is the whole of mankind. He not only represents it, but he is the whole of the human species. He is essentially the whole psyche of mankind. On this actuality various cultures have imposed the illusion that each human being is different. In this illusion mankind has been caught for centuries, and this illusion has become a reality. If you observe closely the whole psychological structure of yourself, you will find that just as you suffer, so does all mankind suffer in various degrees. If you are lonely, the whole of humankind knows this loneliness. Agony, jealousy, envy and fear are known to all. So psychologically, inwardly, you are like another human being. There may be differences physically, biologically – one is tall, or short and so on – but basically you are the representative of all mankind.

So psychologically you are the world. You are responsible for the whole of mankind, not for yourself as a separate human being, which is a psychological illusion. As the representative of the whole human race, your response is whole, not partial. So responsibility has a totally different meaning. One has to learn the art of this responsibility. If one grasps fully the significance of the fact that psychologically one is the world, then responsibility becomes overpowering love. Then one will care for the child, not just at a tender age, but will see that he understands the significance of responsibility throughout his life. This art includes behaviour, the ways of one's thinking and the importance of correct action. In these schools of ours, responsibility to the earth, to nature and to each other is part of our education, not merely emphasis on academic subjects, though they are necessary.

Then we can ask: what is the teacher teaching and what is the pupil receiving? And more widely, what is learning? What is the educator's function? Is it to teach merely algebra and physics or is it to awaken in the student, and so in himself, an enormous sense of responsibility? Can the two go together; that is, the academic subjects which will help in a career and the responsibility for the whole of mankind and life? Or must they be kept separate? If they are separate, then there will be contradiction in the student's life; he will become a hypocrite and unconsciously or deliberately keep his life in two definite compartments. Mankind lives in this division. At home he will be one way, and in the factory or the office he will assume a different face. Is it possible for the two to move together?

When a question of this kind is put, one must investigate the implications of the question and not whether it is or it is not possible. So it is of the greatest importance how you approach this question. If you approach it from your limited background – and all conditioning is limited – then you will have only a partial grasp of the implications in this. You must come to this question afresh. Then you will find the futility of the question itself, because, as you approach it afresh, you will see that these two meet like two streams making a formidable river which is your life, your daily life of total responsibility.

Is this what you are teaching, realizing that the teacher has the greatest of all professions? These are not mere words but an abiding actuality, not to be slurred over. If you do not feel the truth of this, then you really should have another profession, or you will live in the illusions that mankind has created for itself.

So we can again ask: what are you teaching and what is the pupil learning? Are you creating that strange atmosphere in which actual learning takes place? If you have understood the enormousness of responsibility and the beauty of it, then you are totally responsible for the student – for what he wears, what he eats, the manner of his speech, and so on.

From this question arises another: what is learning? Probably most of us have not even asked that question, or if we have asked it, our response has been from tradition, which is accumulated knowledge, knowledge which functions with skill or without skill to earn our daily living. This is what one has been taught, for which all the usual schools, colleges and universities exist. Knowledge predominates, which is one of our greatest conditionings, and so the brain is never free from the known. It is always adding to what is already known, and so the brain is put into a straitjacket of the known and is never free to discover a way of life which may not be based on the known at all. The known makes for a wide or narrow rut, and one remains in that rut thinking there is security in it; but that security is destroyed by the very finite known. This has been the way of human life up to now.

So is there a way of learning which does not make life into a routine, a narrow groove? Then what is learning? We must be very clear about the ways of knowledge. We acquire technological and psychological knowledge, and then act from that knowledge; or we act, and from that action acquire knowledge. Both are acquisition of knowledge. Knowledge is always the past. Is there a way of acting without the enormous weight of man's accumulated knowledge? There is. It is not learning as we have known it; it is pure observation. It is not observation which is continuous and which then becomes memory, but observation from moment to moment. The observer is the essence of knowledge, and he imposes on what he observes that which he has acquired through experience and various forms of sensory reaction. The observer is always manipulating what he observes, and what he observes is always reduced to knowledge. So he is always caught in the old tradition of habit-forming.

So learning is pure observation, not only of the things outside you, but also of that which is happening inwardly – observation without the observer.

7. LEARNING

The whole movement of life is learning

The whole movement of life is learning. There is never a time when there is no learning. Every action is a movement of learning, and every relationship is learning. The accumulation of knowledge, which is called learning and to which we are so accustomed, is necessary to a limited extent, but that limitation prevents us from comprehending ourselves. Knowledge is measurable, more or less, but in learning there is no measure. This is really very important to understand, especially if you are to grasp the full meaning of a religious life. Knowledge is memory, but – if you have observed – the actual, the now is not memory. In observation memory has no place. The actual is what is actually happening now; the second later is measurable and is the way of memory.

If you are interested in observing the movement of an insect or whatever interests you, attention is needed. This attention also is not measurable. It is the responsibility of the educator to understand the whole nature and structure of memory, to observe its limitation, and to help the student to see this. We learn from books or from a teacher who has a great deal of information about a subject, and our brains are filled with this information. This information is about things, about nature, about everything outside of us; and when we want to learn about ourselves we turn to books that tell about ourselves. So this process goes on endlessly, and gradually we become second-hand human beings. This is an observable fact throughout the world. And this is our modern education.

The act of learning, as we have pointed out, is the act of pure observation, and this observation is not held within the limitation of memory. We learn to earn a living but we never live. The capacity to earn a living takes most of our life; we have hardly any time for other things. We find time for gossip, to be entertained, to play, but all this is not living. There is a whole field that is actual living, which is totally neglected.

To learn the art of living one must have leisure. The word leisure is greatly misunderstood. Generally, it means not to be occupied with the usual things we have to do, such as earning a livelihood, going to the office or factory, and so on. Then, only when that is over is there leisure. During that so-called leisure, we want to be amused, we want to relax, we want to do the things that we really like or that demand our highest capacity. Earning a livelihood from whatever we do is in opposition to so-called leisure. So there is always strain, tension and the effort to escape from that tension. Then, leisure is when we have no strain. During that leisure we pick up a newspaper, open a novel, chatter, play, and so on. This is the actual fact. This is what is going on everywhere. Earning a livelihood is the denial of living. Leisure, as it is understood, is a respite from the pressure of livelihood. We generally consider the pressure of earning a living or any pressure imposed on us to be an absence of leisure. There is a much greater pressure in us, conscious or unconscious, which is desire.

School is a place of leisure. It is only when you have leisure that you can learn. That is, learning can take place only when there is no pressure of any kind. When a danger, like a snake, confronts you, there is a kind of learning from the pressure of the fact of that danger. The learning under that pressure is the cultivation of memory, which will help you to recognize future danger, and so it becomes a mechanical response.

Leisure implies that a mind is not occupied. It is only then that there is a state of learning. School is a place of learning, and not merely a place for accumulating knowledge. This is really important to understand. As we said, knowledge is necessary and has its own limited place in life. Unfortunately, this limitation has devoured all our lives, and we have no space for learning. We are so occupied with earning our livelihood that it takes all the energy of the mechanism of thought, so that we are exhausted at the end of the day and need to be stimulated. We recover from this exhaustion through entertainment – religious or otherwise. This is the life of human beings. Human beings have created a society which demands all their time, all their energies, all their life. There is no leisure to learn, and so life becomes mechanical, almost meaningless. So we must be very clear in the understanding of the word leisure: it is a time, a period when the mind is not occupied with anything whatsoever. It is the time of observation. It is only the unoccupied mind that can observe. Free observation is the movement of learning. This frees the mind from being mechanical.

So can the teacher, the educator, help the student to understand this whole business of earning a livelihood with all its pressure, the learning that helps you to acquire a job with all the accompanying fears and anxieties and looking on tomorrow with dread? Because the teacher has understood the nature of leisure and pure observation, can the teacher help the student to have a non-mechanical mind, so that earning a livelihood does not become a torture, a great travail throughout life?

It is the absolute responsibility of the teacher to cultivate the flowering of goodness in leisure. For this reason the schools exist. It is the responsibility of the teacher to create a new generation, to change the social structure from its total preoccupation with earning a livelihood. Then teaching becomes a holy act.

8. RADICAL CHANGE

Education is the cultivation
of total responsibility

In past letters we have said that total responsibility is love. This responsibility is not for a particular nation or a particular group or community, or for a particular deity, or some form of political programme, or for your own guru, but for all mankind. To have this deeply understood and felt is the responsibility of the educator.

Almost all of us feel responsible for our families and children, but we do not have the feeling of being wholly concerned and committed to the environment around us, to nature, or of being totally responsible for our actions. That absolute care is love. Without this love, there can be no change in society. The idealists, though they may love their ideal or their concept, have not brought about a radically different society. Revolutionaries, terrorists, have not fundamentally changed the pattern of our societies. Physically violent revolutionaries have talked about freedom for all men, forming a new society, but all the jargon and slogans have only further tortured the spirit and existence. They have twisted words to suit their own limited outlooks. No form of violence has changed society in the most fundamental way. Great rulers, through the authority of a few, have brought about some kind of order in society. Even the totalitarians have established, through violence and torture, a superficial semblance of order. We are not talking about such an order in society.

We are saying very definitely and most emphatically that it is only having a sense of total responsibility for all mankind, which is love, that can basically transform the present state of society. Existing systems in various parts of the world are corrupt, degenerate and wholly immoral. You have only to look around you to see this fact. Millions upon millions are spent on armaments throughout the world; the politicians talk about peace while preparing for war. Religions have declared over and over again the sanctity of peace, but

33

they have encouraged wars and subtle kinds of violence and torture. There are innumerable divisions and sects with their rituals and all the nonsense that goes on in the name of God and religion. Where there is division there must be disorder, struggle and conflict, whether the division is religious, political or economic. Our modern society is based on greed, envy and power.

When you consider all this as it actually is, this overpowering commercialism indicates degeneration and basic immorality. We are destroying the earth and all the things on it for our gratification. To radically change this pattern of our life, which is the basis of all society, is the educator's responsibility.

Education is not merely the teaching of various academic subjects; it is also the cultivation of total responsibility in the student. People do not realize that an educator is bringing into being a new generation. Most schools are concerned only with imparting knowledge; they are not at all concerned with the transformation of man and his daily life. You, the educator in these schools, need to have this deep concern and the care of this total responsibility.

In what manner then can you help the student to feel this quality of love with all its excellence? If you do not feel this yourself, profoundly, talking about responsibility is meaningless. Can you as an educator feel the truth of this? Seeing the truth of it will bring about naturally this love and total responsibility. You have to ponder over it, observe it daily in your life, in your relations with your wife, your friends, your students. And in your relationship with the students you will talk about this from your heart, not pursue mere verbal clarity. The feeling for this reality is the greatest gift that man can have. Once it is burning in you, you will find the right word, right action and correct behaviour. When you consider the student, you will see that he comes to you totally unprepared for all this. He comes to you frightened, nervous, anxious to please or on the defensive, conditioned by his parents and the society in which he has lived his few years. You have to see his background; you have to be concerned with what he actually is and not impose your own opinions, conclusions and judgements on him. Considering what he is will reveal what you are, and so you will find that the student is you.

Now, can you, in the teaching of mathematics, physics, and so on – which he must know, for that is the way of earning a livelihood – convey to the student that he is responsible for the whole of mankind? So that, though he may be working for his own career, his own way of life, it will not make his mind narrow, and he will see the danger of specialization with all its limitations and strange brutality. You have to help him to see all this. The flowering of goodness does not lie in knowing mathematics and biology or in passing examinations and having a successful career. It exists outside these. When there is this flowering, career and other necessary activities are touched by its beauty. Now we lay emphasis on one thing and disregard the flowering entirely.

In these schools we are trying to bring these two together, not artificially, not as a principle or pattern for you to follow, but because you see the absolute truth that these two must flow together for the regeneration of man. Can you do this? Not because you all agree to do it after discussing and coming to a conclusion, but because you see with an inward eye the extraordinary gravity of this; see it for yourself. Then what you say will have significance. Then you become a centre of light not lit by another. As you are all of humanity – which is an actuality, not a verbal statement – you are utterly responsible for the future of man.

Please do not consider this a burden. If you do, it is a bundle of words without any reality; it is an illusion. This responsibility has its own gaiety, its own humour, its own movement without the weight of thought.

9. DILIGENCE

Freedom from self-occupation
brings abundant energy

As we are concerned with education, there are two factors we must bear in mind at all times. One is diligence and the other is negligence. Most religions have talked about the need for the activity of the mind to be controlled, shaped by "the will of God", or by some exterior agency. Devotion to some deity made by the hand or by the mind needs a certain quality of attention in which emotion, sentiment and romantic imagination are involved. This is the activity of the mind, which is thought. The word diligence implies care, watchfulness, observation and a deep sense of freedom. Devotion to an object, a person, or a principle denies this freedom. Diligence is attention which brings about naturally infinite care, concern and the freshness of affection. All this demands great sensitivity. One is sensitive to one's own desires or psychological wounds, or one is sensitive to a particular person, watching his desires and responding quickly to his needs; but that kind of sensitivity is limited and can hardly be called sensitive. The quality of sensitivity of which we are talking comes about naturally when there is total responsibility which is love. Diligence has this quality.

Negligence is indifference, sloth – indifference towards the physical organism, towards the psychological state, and indifference to others. In indifference there is callousness. In this state the mind becomes sluggish, the activity of thought slows down, quickness of perception is denied, and sensitivity is a thing that is incomprehensible. Most of us are sometimes diligent, but most often negligent. They are not really opposites; if they were, diligence would still be negligence.

Most people are "diligent" in their own self-interest, whether that self-interest is identified with the family, with a particular group, sect, or nation. In this self-interest there is the seed of negligence, although there is constant preoccupation with oneself. This preoccupation is limited and so it is negligence. This preoccupation is energy held within a narrow boundary. Diligence is freedom from self-occupation and brings an abundance of energy. When one understands the nature of negligence, the other comes into being without any struggle. When this is fully understood – not just the verbal definitions of negligence and diligence – then the highest excellence in our thought, action, behaviour will manifest itself.

But unfortunately we never demand of ourselves the highest quality of thought, action and behaviour. We hardly ever challenge ourselves, and if we ever do, we have various excuses for not responding fully. Doesn't this indicate an indolence of mind, the feeble activity of thought? The body can be lazy, but never the mind with its quickness of thought and subtlety. Laziness of the body can easily be understood. This laziness may be because one is overworked or overindulged, or has played games too hard. So the body requires rest – which may be considered laziness, though it is not. The watchful mind, being alert, sensitive, knows when the organism needs rest and care.

In our schools it is important to understand that the quality of energy which is diligence requires the right kind of food, the right kind of exercise, and enough sleep. Habit, routine, is the enemy of diligence – habit of thought, of action, of conduct. Thought itself creates its own pattern and lives within it. When that pattern is challenged, either it is disregarded or thought creates another pattern of security. This is the movement of thought – from one pattern to another, from one conclusion, one belief, to another. This is the very negligence of thought. The mind that is diligent has no habit; it has no pattern of response. It is endless movement, never coalescing into habit, never being caught in conclusions. Movement has great depth and volume when it has no boundary brought about by the negligence of thought.

As we are concerned with education, in what manner can the teacher convey this diligence with its sensitivity, with its abundant care in which laziness of the spirit has no place? Of course it is understood that the educator is concerned with this question and sees the importance of diligence throughout the days of his life. If he is, then how will he set about cultivating the flower of diligence? Is he deeply concerned with the student? Does he really take total responsibility for the young people who are in his charge? Or is he there merely to earn a livelihood? As we have pointed out, teaching is the highest capacity of man. You are there and you have the students in front of you. Is it that you are indifferent? Is it that your own personal troubles at home are wasting your energy?

To carry psychological problems from day to day is an utter waste of time and energy, indicating negligence. A diligent mind meets a problem as it arises, observes the nature of it and resolves it immediately. The carrying over of a psychological problem does not resolve the problem. It is a waste of energy and spirit. When you solve problems as they arise, then you will find there are no problems at all.

So, as an educator in these or any other schools, can you cultivate this diligence? It is only in this that the flowering of goodness comes into being. To do this is your total, irrevocable responsibility; and in it is the love which will naturally find a way of helping the student.

10. SECURITY

The school is the student's home

It is important that the teacher should feel economically and psychologically secure in these schools. Some teachers may be willing to teach without much concern for their economic position; they may have come for the teachings and for psychological reasons, but every teacher should feel secure in the sense of being at home, cared for, without financial worries. If the teacher does not feel secure and therefore is not free to give attention to the student and the student's security, he will not be able to be totally responsible. If the teacher is not happy, his attention will be divided and he will be incapable of exercising his entire capacity.

So it is important to choose the right teachers, inviting each one to stay for some time at our schools to find out whether he or she can happily join in what is being done. This must be mutual. Then the teacher, being happy, secure, feeling that he or she is at home, can create in the student this sense of security, the feeling that the school is the student's home.

Feeling at home implies that there is no sense of fear, that the student is protected physically, cared for and free. Although the student may object to the idea of being protected, guarded, it does not mean that he is held in a prison, confined and watched critically. Freedom obviously does not mean to do what one likes, and it is equally obvious that one can never totally do what one likes. The attempt to do what one likes – so-called individual freedom, which is to choose a course of action according to one's desire – has brought about social and economic confusion in the world. The reaction to this confusion is totalitarianism.

Freedom is a very complex affair. One must approach it with utmost attention, for freedom is not the opposite of bondage, or an escape from the circumstances in which one is caught. It is not from something, or avoidance of constraint. Freedom has no opposite; it is of itself. The very understanding of the nature of freedom is the awakening of intelligence. It is not an adjustment to what is, but the understanding of what is and so going beyond it. If the teacher does not understand the nature of freedom, he will only impose his prejudices, his limitations, his conclusions on the student. The student will naturally resist or accept this through fear, becoming a conventional human being, whether timid or aggressive. It is only in the understanding of this freedom of living – not the idea of it or the verbal acceptance of it, which becomes a slogan – that the mind is free to learn.

A school, after all, is a place where the student is basically happy, not bullied, not frightened by examinations, not compelled to act according to a pattern, a system. It is a place where the art of learning is being taught. If the student is not happy he is incapable of learning this art.

Memorizing, recording information, is considered learning. This brings about a mind that is limited and therefore heavily conditioned. The art of learning is to give the right place to information, to act skilfully according to what is learnt, but at the same time not to be bound psychologically by the limitations of knowledge and the images or symbols that thought creates. Art implies putting everything in its right place – but not according to some ideal. To understand the mechanism of ideals and conclusions is to learn the art of observation. A concept put together by thought, either for the future or according to the past, is an ideal; it is an idea projected or a remembrance. It is a shadow-play, making an abstraction of the actual. This abstraction is an avoidance of what is happening now. This escape from the fact is unhappiness.

Now, can we as teachers help the student to be happy in the real sense? Can we help him to be concerned with what is actually going on? This is attention. The student watching a leaf fluttering in the sun is being attentive. To force him back to the book at that moment is to discourage attention; whereas to help him to watch that leaf fully makes him aware of the depth of attention in which there is no distraction. In the same way, because he has just seen what attention implies, he will be able to turn to the book or whatever is being taught. In this attention there is no compulsion, no conformity. It is the freedom in which there is total observation. Can the teacher himself have this quality of attention? Then only can he help another.

For the most part we struggle against distractions, but there are no distractions. Suppose you daydream or your mind is wandering, that is what is actually taking place. Observe that. That observation is attention. So there is no distraction.

Can this be taught to the students? Can this art be learnt? You are totally responsible for the student. You must create this atmosphere of learning, a seriousness in which there is a sense of freedom and happiness.

11. COMPARISON

Imitation corrupts the mind

As we have already pointed out several times in these letters, the schools exist primarily to bring about a profound transformation in human beings. The educator is wholly responsible for this. Unless the teacher realizes this central factor, he will be merely instructing the student to become a businessman, an engineer, a lawyer, or a politician. There are so many of these who seem to be incapable of transforming either themselves or their society. Perhaps in the present structure of society lawyers and businessmen may be necessary, but when these schools came into being the intention was, and remains, to transform humanity profoundly. The teachers in these schools should really understand this, not intellectually, not as an idea, but because they see the full implications of this with their whole being. We are concerned with the total development of a human being, not merely with accumulating knowledge.

Ideas and ideals are one thing, and fact, the actual happening, is another. The two can never come together. Ideals have been imposed upon facts, and they twist what is happening to conform to what should be, the ideal. The utopia is a conclusion drawn from what is happening, and sacrifices the actual to conform to that which has been idealized. This has been the process for millennia, and every student and all the intellectuals revel in ideations. The avoidance of what is is the beginning of the corruption of the mind. This corruption pervades all religions, politics and education, all human relationship. The understanding of this process of avoidance and going beyond it is our concern.

Ideals corrupt the mind; they are born of ideas, judgements and hope. Ideas are abstractions from what is, and any idea or conclusion about what is actually happening distorts what is happening, and so corruption takes place. It takes attention away from the fact, from what is, and so directs attention to the fanciful. This movement away from the fact makes for symbols, images, which then take on all-consuming importance. This movement away from the fact is corruption of the mind. Human beings indulge in this movement in conversation, in their relationships, in almost everything they do. The fact is instantly translated into an idea or a conclusion, which then dictates our reactions. When something is seen, thought immediately makes a counterpart and that becomes the real. You see a dog, and instantly thought turns to whatever image you may have about dogs, and so you never see the dog.

Can the students be taught to remain with the fact, the actual happening now, whether it is psychologically or externally? Knowledge is not the fact; it is about the fact, and that has its proper place, but knowledge prevents the perception of what actually is. Then corruption takes place. This is really very important to understand. Ideals are considered noble, exalted, of great purposeful significance, and what is actually happening is considered merely sensory, worldly and of lesser value. Schools the world over have some exalted purpose, ideal; so they are educating the students in corruption.

What corrupts the mind? We are using the word mind to imply the senses, the capacity to think, and the brain that stores all memories and experiences as knowledge. This total movement is the mind. The conscious as well as the unconscious, the so-called superconsciousness, the whole of this is the mind. We are asking what the factors, the seeds of corruption are in all this. We said ideals corrupt. Knowledge also corrupts the mind. Knowledge, particular or extensive, is the movement of the past, and when the past overshadows the actual, corruption takes place. Knowledge, projected into the future and directing what is happening now, is corruption. We are using the word corruption to mean that which is being broken up, that which is not taken as a whole. The fact can never be broken up; the fact can never be limited by knowledge. The completeness of the fact opens the door to infinity. Completeness cannot be divided; it is not self-contradictory; it cannot divide itself. Completeness, wholeness, is infinite movement.

Imitation, conformity, is one of the great factors of corruption of the mind. The example – the hero, the saviour, the guru – is the most destructive factor of corruption. To follow, to obey, to conform, denies freedom. Freedom is from the beginning, not at the end. It is not to conform, to imitate, accept first, and then eventually find freedom. That is the spirit of totalitarianism; that is the cruelty, the ruthlessness of the dictator, of the authority, of the guru or of the priest.

So authority is corruption. Authority is the breaking-up of integrity, the whole, the complete, whether it is the authority of a teacher in a school or the authority of an institution or the authority of a purpose, of an ideal, of the one who says 'I know'. The pressure of authority in any form is the distorting factor of corruption. Authority basically denies freedom. It is the function of a true teacher to instruct, point out, inform, without the corrupting influence of authority.

The authority of comparison destroys. When one student is compared with another, both are being hurt. To live without comparison is to have integrity. Will you, the teacher, do this?

12. PSYCHOLOGICAL WOUNDS

Education is to free the mind
of the limited energy of the "me"

It seems that human beings have enormous amounts of energy. They have been to the moon, have climbed the highest peaks of the earth. They have had prodigious energy for wars, for the instruments of war, and great energy for technological development. Mankind has had energy to accumulate vast knowledge, to build the pyramids, to explore the atom, and to work every day. When one considers all this, it is striking to realize the energy expended. This energy has gone into the investigation of external things, but man has given very little energy to inquire into the whole psychological structure of himself. Energy is needed, both externally and inwardly to act – or to be totally silent.

Action and non-action require great energy. We have used "positive" energy in wars, in writing books, in performing surgery, and to work beneath the seas. Non-action requires far more than the so-called positive action. Positive action is to control, to support, to escape. Non-action is the total attention of observation. In this observation, that which is being observed undergoes a transformation. This silent observation demands not only physical energy, but also deep psychological energy. We are used to the former, and this conditioning limits our energy. In a complete, silent observation, which is non-action, there is no expenditure of energy, and so energy is limitless.

Non-action is not the opposite of action. Going to work daily, year after year for so many years, which may be necessary as things are, does limit; but not-working does not mean you will have boundless energy. The very slothfulness of the mind is a waste of energy, as is the laziness of the body. Our education in every field narrows down this energy. Our way of life, which is a constant struggle to become or not to become, is the dissipation of energy.

Energy is timeless and is not to be measured, but our actions are measurable, and so we bring down this limitless energy to the narrow circle of the "me". Having confined it, we then search for the immeasurable. This searching is part of positive action, and is therefore a waste of psychological energy. So there is a never-ending movement within the archives of the "me".

What we are concerned with in education is to free the mind of the "me". As we have said on several occasions in these letters, it is our function to bring about a new generation free of this limited energy which is called the "me". It must be repeated again that these schools exist to bring this about.

In a previous letter we talked about the corruption of the mind. The root of this corruption is the "me". The "me" is the image, the picture, the word that is passed from generation to generation; and one has to contend with the weight of tradition of the "me". It is the fact that is to be observed, not the consequence of the fact or how the fact has come into being; the latter are fairly easy to explain, but to observe the fact with all its reactions, without motive which distorts the fact, is negative action. This then transforms the fact. It is important to understand this very deeply – not to act upon the fact, but to observe what is.

Every human being is wounded both psychologically and physically. It is comparatively easy to deal with the physical pain, but the psychological pain remains hidden. The consequence of the psychological wound is to build a wall around oneself, to resist further pain and so become fearful or withdraw into isolation. The wound has been caused by the image of the "me" with its limited energy. Because it is limited, it is hurt. That which is not measurable can never be damaged, can never be corrupted. Anything that is limited can be hurt, but that which is whole is beyond the reach of thought.

Can the educator help the student never to be psychologically wounded, not only while he is part of the school but throughout his life? If the educator sees the great damage that comes from this wounding, then how will he educate the student? What will he actually do to see that the student is never hurt throughout his life?

The student comes to the school already having been hurt. Probably he is unaware of this hurt. The teacher, by observing the student's reactions, his fears and aggressiveness, will discover the damage that has been done. So he has two problems: to free the student from past damage and prevent future wounds.

Is this your concern? Or do you merely read this letter, understand it intellectually, which is no understanding at all, and so are not concerned with the student? If you are concerned, as you should be, what will you do with the fact that he is wounded and that you must prevent at all costs any further hurts? How do you approach this problem? What is the state of your mind when you face this problem? It is also your problem, not only the student's. You are hurt and so is the student. So you are both concerned, it is not a one-sided problem; you are as much involved as the student. This involvement is the central factor that you must face, observe. Merely to have a desire to be free of your past wounds, and to hope never to be hurt again, is a waste of energy. Complete attention, the observation of this fact, will not only tell the story of the wound itself, but the very attention dispels, wipes away the hurt. So attention is the vast energy which can never be wounded or corrupted.

Please do not accept what is said in these letters. Acceptance is the destruction of truth. Test it, not at some future date, but test it as you read this letter. When you test it, not casually but with all your heart and being, then you will discover for yourself the truth of the matter. And then only will you be able to help the student to wipe away the past and have a mind that is incapable of being hurt.

13. HABIT

Habit makes the mind insensitive

These letters are written in a friendly spirit. They are not intended to dominate your way of thinking or to persuade you to conform to the way the writer thinks or feels. They are not propaganda. It is really a dialogue between you and the writer like two friends talking over their problems, and in good friendship there is never any sense of competition or domination. You, too, must have observed the state of the world and our society and seen that there must be a radical transformation in the way human beings live, in their relation to each other, their relation with the world as a whole, and in every way possible. We are talking to each other, both being deeply concerned not only with our own particular selves, but also with the students for whom you are wholly responsible.

The teacher is the most important person in a school, for on her or him depends the future welfare of mankind. This is not a mere verbal statement. This is an absolute and irrevocable fact. Only when the educator himself feels the dignity and the respect implicit in his work will he be aware that teaching is the highest calling, greater than that of the politician, greater than that of the princes of the world. The writer means every word of this, so please do not brush it aside as an exaggeration or an attempt to make you feel a false importance. You and the students must flower together in goodness.

We have been pointing out the corrupting or degenerating factors of the mind. As society is disintegrating, these schools must be centres for the regeneration of the mind. Not of thought. Thought can never be regenerated, for thought is always limited; but the regeneration of the totality of the mind is possible. This possibility is not conceptual but actual when one has examined deeply the ways of the degeneration. In previous letters we have explored some of these ways.

We must now investigate the destructive nature of tradition, of habit and the repetitive ways of thought. To follow, accepting tradition, seems to give a certain security to one's life, to the outer life as well as the inner. The search for security in every possible way has been the motive, the driving power of most of our actions. The demand for psychological security overshadows that for physical security and so makes physical security uncertain. This psychological security is the basis of tradition passed on from one generation to another through words, through rituals, beliefs – whether religious, political or sociological. We seldom question the accepted norm, but when we do question we invariably fall into a trap in a new pattern. This has been our way of life: reject one thing and accept another. The new is more enticing and the old is left to the passing generation; but both generations are caught in patterns, in systems. This is the movement of tradition. The very word implies conformity, whether the tradition is modern or ancient. There is no good or bad tradition, there is only tradition, the vain repetition of ritual in all the churches, temples and mosques. They are utterly meaningless, but emotion, sentiment, romanticism, imagination lend them colour and illusion. This is the nature of superstition, and every priest in the world encourages it. This process of indulging in things that have no meaning, or investing in things that have no significance, is a waste of energy, which degenerates the mind. One has to be deeply aware of these facts. That very attention dissolves all illusions.

Then there is habit. There are no good or bad habits, only habit. Habit implies a repetitive action which arises from not being aware. One falls into habits deliberately, or is persuaded through propaganda; or, being afraid, one falls into self-protective reflexes. It is the same with pleasure. Following a routine, however effective or necessary it may be in daily life, generally leads to a mechanical way of living. One can do the same thing at the same hour every day without it becoming a habit, when there is an awareness of what is being done. Attention dispels habit. It is only when there is no attention that habits are formed. You can get up at the same time every morning and you know why you are getting up. This awareness may appear to another as a habit, good or bad, but actually for the one who is aware, is attentive, there is no habit at all. We fall into psychological habits or routine because we think it is the most comfortable way of living. When you observe closely, even with the habits formed in relationships, personal or otherwise, there is a certain quality of indolence, carelessness and disregard. All this gives a false sense of intimacy, security and leads to facile cruelty.

There is danger in every habit – the habit of smoking, repetitive action, in the employment of words, thought or behaviour. This makes the mind utterly insensitive; and the degenerating process is to find some form of illusory security such as a nation, a belief or an ideal and cling to it. All these factors are very destructive to real security. We live in a make-believe world, which has become a reality. To question this illusion is to become either a revolutionary or to embrace permissiveness. Both these are factors of degeneration.

After all, the brain with its extraordinary capacities has been conditioned from generation to generation into accepting this fallacious security, which has now become a deep-rooted habit. To break down this habit, we go through various forms of torture, multiple escapes, or throw ourselves into some idealistic utopia. It is the problem of the educator to investigate, and his creative capacity lies in observing very closely his deep-rooted conditioning and that of the student. This is a mutual process; it is not that you investigate your conditioning first and then inform the other of your discoveries. You explore together and find the truth of the matter. This demands a certain quality of patience, not the patience of time but perseverance, and the diligent care of total responsibility.

14. BEAUTY

The movement of thought is not beauty

We have become far too clever. Our brains have been trained to be verbally, intellectually, very bright. They are crammed with a great deal of information, and we use this for profitable careers. A clever, intellectual person is praised, shown honour. Such people seem to usurp all the important places in the world; they have power, position, prestige; but their cleverness betrays them at the end. In their hearts they never know what love is or deep charity and generosity, for they are enclosed in their vanity and arrogance. This has become the pattern of all highly endowed schools. A boy or girl in a conventional school gets trapped in modern civilization and is lost to the whole beauty of life.

When you wander through woods with heavy shadows and dappled light and suddenly come upon an open space, a green meadow surrounded by stately trees, or a sparkling stream, you wonder why man has lost his relationship to nature and the beauty of the earth, the fallen leaf and the broken branch. If you have lost touch with nature, then you will inevitably lose relationship with another. Nature is not just the flowers, the lovely green lawn or the flowing waters in your little garden, but the whole earth with all the things on it. We consider that nature exists for our use, for our convenience, and so lose communion with the earth. Sensitivity to the fallen leaf and to the tall tree on a hill is far more important than all the passing of examinations and having a bright career. Those are not the whole of life. Life is like a vast river with a great volume of water without a beginning or an ending. We take out of that fast-running current a bucket of water, and that confined water becomes our life. This is our conditioning and our everlasting sorrow.

The movement of thought is not beauty. Thought can create what appears to be beautiful – the painting, the marble figure or a lovely poem – but this is not beauty. Beauty is supreme sensitivity, not to the sense of one's own pains and anxieties, but encompassing the whole existence of humanity. There is beauty only when the current of the "me" has completely dried up. When the "me" is not, beauty is. With the abandonment of the self, the passion of beauty comes into being.

We have been talking over together in these letters the degeneration of the mind. We have pointed out for your examination and investigation some of the ways of this deterioration. One of its basic activities is thought. Thought is a breaking-up of the wholeness of the mind. The whole contains the part, but the part can never be that which is complete. Thought is the most active part of our life. Feeling goes with thought. Essentially they are one, though we tend to separate them. Having separated them, we give great importance to feeling, to sentiment, to romanticism and devotion; but thought, like a string in a necklace, weaves itself through them all, hidden, alive, controlling and shaping. It is always there, though we like to think our deep emotions are essentially different. In this lies great illusion, a deception that is highly regarded and leads to dishonesty.

As we have said, thought is the actuality of our daily life. All so-called sacred books are the product of thought. They may be revered as revelation, but they are essentially thought. Thought has put together the turbine and the great temples of the earth, the rocket, and the enmity in men. Thought has been responsible for wars, for the language one uses and the image made by the hand or by the mind. Thought dominates relationship. Thought has described what love is, the heavens and the pain of misery. Man worships thought, admires its subtleties, its cunning, its violence, its cruelties in the name of a cause. Thought has brought great advances in technology and with them a capacity for destruction. This has been the story of thought, repeated throughout the centuries.

Why has humanity given such extraordinary importance to thought? Is it because, even though it is activated through the senses, it is the only thing we have? Is it because thought has been able to dominate nature, dominate its surroundings, and has brought about some physical security? Is it because it is the greatest instrument through which man operates, lives and benefits? Is it because thought has made the gods, the saviours, the super-consciousness – forgetting the anxiety, the fear, the sorrow, the envy, the guilt? Is it because it holds people together as nations, as groups, as sects? Is it because it offers hope to dark lives? Is it because it gives an opening to escape from the daily boring ways of our lives? Is it because, not knowing what the future is, it offers the security of the past, in its arrogant insistence on experience? Is it because there is stability in knowledge, the avoidance of fear in the certainty of the known? Is it because thought in itself has assumed an invulnerable position, taken a stand against the unknown? Is it because love is unaccountable, not measurable, while thought is measured and resists the changeless movement of love?

We have never questioned the very nature of thought. We have accepted thought as inevitable as our eyes and legs. We have never probed to the very depth of thought, and because we have never questioned it, it has assumed pre-eminence. It is the tyrant of our life, and tyrants are rarely challenged.

So, as educators, we are going to expose it to the bright light of observation. The light of observation not only instantly dispels illusion, but the clarity of its light reveals the tiniest detail of that which is being observed. As we have said, observation is not from a fixed point, from a belief, prejudice or conclusion. Opinion is a rather shoddy affair and so also is experience. The man of experience is a dangerous person because he is caught in the prison of his own knowledge.

So can you observe with extraordinary clarity the whole movement of thought? This light is freedom. This does not mean that you have captured it and employed it for your convenience and benefit. The very observation of thought is the observation of your whole being, and this very being is put together by thought. As thought is finite, limited, so are you.

15. CAPACITY

Capacity is limited by desire

We are still concerned with the wholeness of the mind. The mind includes the senses, the erratic emotions, the capacity of the brain and ever-restless thought. All this is the mind, including various attributes of consciousness. When the whole mind is in operation, it is boundless; it has great energy and action without the shadow of regret and promise of reward. This quality of mind, this wholeness, is intelligence. Can this be conveyed to the student and can she or he be helped to grasp its significance quickly? Surely it is the responsibility of the educator to bring this about.

The capacity of thought is shaped and controlled by desire, so the capacity is narrowed down. This capacity is limited by the movement of desire. Desire is the essence of sensation. Ambition limits the capacity of the brain, which is thought. This capacity is restricted by social and economic demands or by one's own experience and motive. It is narrowed down by an ideal, by the sanctions of various religious beliefs, by unending fear. Fear is not separate from pleasure.

Desire, the essence of sensation, is shaped by environment, by tradition, by our own inclinations and temperament, and thus capacity or action that demands total energy is conditioned according to our comfort and pleasure. Desire is a compelling factor in our lives, not to be suppressed or evaded, not to be cajoled and reasoned with, but rather to be understood. This understanding can come into being only through the investigation of desire and the observation of its movement. Knowing the impelling fire of desire, most religious and sectarian prohibitions have made it into something that must be suppressed, controlled or surrendered – handed over as it were – to a deity or principle. The innumerable vows that people have taken to deny desire totally have in no way burnt it out. It is there.

So we must approach it differently, bearing in mind that intelligence is not awakened by desire. A desire to go to the moon brings about enormous technical knowledge, but that knowledge is limited intelligence. Knowledge is always specialized and therefore incomplete; but we are talking of intelligence, which is the movement of the wholeness of the mind. It is with this intelligence that we are concerned and with the awakening of it in both the educator and the student.

As we said earlier, capacity is limited by desire. Desire is sensation: the sensation of new experiences, of new forms of excitement, the sensation of climbing the highest peaks on earth, the sensation of power, of status. All this limits the energy of the brain. Desire gives the illusion of security, and the brain, which needs security, encourages and sustains every form of desire. If we do not understand the place of desire, it brings about degeneration of the mind. This is really important to understand. Thought is the movement of this desire. Curiosity to discover is urged on by a desire for greater sensations and the illusory certainty of security. Curiosity has brought the enormous amount of knowledge which has its importance in our daily life. Curiosity has significance in observation.

Thought may be the central factor of degeneration of the mind, whereas insight opens the door to the wholeness of action. We will go into the full meaning of insight in another letter but for now we must consider whether thought is destructive to the wholeness of the mind. We have made the statement that it is, but do not accept it until you have thoroughly, freely examined it.

What we mean by wholeness of the mind is infinite capacity and total emptiness in which there is immeasurable energy. Thought, by its very nature being limited, imposes its narrowness on the whole, and so thought is always in the forefront. Thought is limited because it is the outcome of memory and knowledge accumulated through experience. Knowledge is the past; that which has been is always limited. Remembrance may project a future, but that future is tied to the past. So thought is always limited. Thought is measurable – the more and the less, the larger and the smaller. This measurement is the movement of time: I have been, I shall be. When thought predominates, however subtly, cunningly and vitally, it perverts wholeness. But we have given to thought the greatest importance.

If one may ask, after having read this letter, have you grasped the significance of the nature of thought and the wholeness of the mind? If you have, can you convey this to the student, who is your total responsibility? This is a difficult matter. If you have no light you cannot help another to have it. You may explain very clearly or define it in chosen words, but it will not have the passion of truth.

16. INSIGHT AND HONESTY

Which is the honest desire or thought, and which is not?

Any form of conflict, struggle, corrupts the mind – the mind being the wholeness of all our existence. This quality is destroyed when there is any kind of friction, any kind of contradiction. As most of us live in a perpetual state of contradiction and conflict, this lack of completeness makes for degeneration. We are concerned here to discover for ourselves whether it is at all possible to end these degenerating factors.

Perhaps most of us have never thought about this; we have accepted it as a normal way of life. We have convinced ourselves that conflict, like competition, brings growth, and we have various explanations for this – the tree struggles in the forest for light; the baby just born struggles for breath; the mother labours to deliver. We are conditioned to accept this and to live in this manner. This has been the way of our life for generations, and any suggestion that perhaps there might be a way of life without conflict seems quite incredible. You may listen to this as some idealistic nonsense, or reject it out of hand, but you never consider whether there is any significance in the statement that it is possible to live a life without a shadow of conflict. When you are concerned with integrity and the responsibility of bringing about a new generation, which as educators is the only function you have, can you investigate this fact? And in the very process of educating, can you convey to the student what you are discovering for yourself?

Conflict in any form is an indication of resistance. In a fast-flowing river there is no resistance; it flows around big boulders, through villages and towns. Man controls it for his own purpose. After all, doesn't freedom imply absence of the resistance that thought has built around itself?

Honesty is a very complex affair. When one says to oneself that one must be honest, is that possible? What are you honest about and for what reason? Can you be honest with yourself and so be fair to another? Is honesty a matter of ideals? Can an idealist ever be honest? He is living in a future carved out of the past; he is caught between that which has been and that which ought to be, and so he can never be honest. You are the centre of various sometimes contradictory activities, of various thoughts, feelings and desires which are always in opposition to each other. Which is the honest desire or thought, and which is not? These are not mere rhetorical questions or clever arguments. It is very important to find out what it means to be totally honest, because we are going to deal with insight and the immediacy of action. It is utterly important, if we would grasp the depth of meaning of insight, to have the quality of complete integrity, to have that integrity which is the honesty of the whole.

One may feel honest about an ideal, a principle or an ingrained belief. Surely this is not honesty. Honesty can be only when there is no conflict of duality, when the opposite does not exist. There is darkness and light, night and day; there is man, woman, the tall, the short, and so on, but it is thought that makes them opposites, puts them in contradiction. We are expressing the psychological contradiction that mankind has cultivated. Love is not the opposite of hate or jealousy. If it were, it would not be love. Humility is not the opposite of vanity or pride and arrogance. If it were, it would still be part of arrogance and pride and so could not be humility. Humility is totally divorced from all this. A mind that is humble is unaware of its humility. So honesty is not the opposite of dishonesty.

One can be sincere in one's belief or in one's concept, but that sincerity breeds conflict; and where there is conflict there is no honesty. So we are asking if you can be honest to yourself. Yourself is a mixture of many movements crossing each other, dominating each other and rarely flowing together. When all these movements flow together, then there is honesty. There is separation between the conscious and unconscious, God and the devil. Thought has brought about these divisions and the conflict that exists between these divisions. Goodness has no opposite.

With this new understanding of what honesty is, we can proceed with the investigation into what insight is. This is utterly important because that may be the factor to revolutionize our action and bring about a transformation in the brain itself. We have said that our way of life has become mechanical – the past with all the accumulated experience and knowledge, which is the source of thought, is directing, shaping all action. The past and the future are interrelated and inseparable, and the very process of thinking is based upon this. Thought is ever-limited, finite. Though it may pretend to reach heaven, that very heaven is within the frame of thought. Memory is measurable, as time is. This movement of thought can never be fresh, new, original. So action based on thought must ever be broken up, incomplete, contradictory. This whole movement of thought must be deeply understood, including its place relative to seeing to the necessities of life and things that must be remembered. Then what is action which is not the continuance of remembrance? It is insight.

Insight is not the careful deduction of thought, the analytical process of thought or the time-binding nature of memory. It is instantaneous perception without the perceiver. From this insight, action takes place. From this insight the explanation of any problem is accurate, final and true. There are no regrets, no reactions. It is absolute. There can be no insight without the quality of love. Insight is not an intellectual affair to be argued about. This love is the highest form of sensitivity when all the senses are flowering together. Without this sensitivity – which is not to one's desires, problems and all the pettiness of life – insight is obviously quite impossible.

Insight is holistic. Holistic implies the whole, the whole of the mind. The mind is all the experience of humanity, including the vast accumulated knowledge with its technical skills, with its sorrows, anxiety, pain, grief and loneliness. But insight is beyond all this. Freedom from sorrow, from grief, from loneliness is essential for isight to be. Insight is not a continuous movement. It cannot be captured by thought. Insight is supreme intelligence, and this intelligence employs thought as a tool. Insight is intelligence with its beauty and love; they are really inseparable; they are actually one. This is the whole, which is the most sacred.

17. DESIRE AND DISORDER

Can the senses be supremely active
without desire coming in?

School is where one learns not only the knowledge required for daily life but also the art of living with all its complexities and subtleties. We seem to forget this and become totally caught up in the superficiality of knowledge. Knowledge is always superficial. Learning the art of living is not considered to be necessary; living is not considered to be an art.

When one leaves school, one stops learning, and continues to live on that which one has accumulated as knowledge. We never consider that life is a whole process of learning. As one observes life, daily living is a constant change and movement, and one's mind is not quick and sensitive enough to follow its subtleties. One comes to it with ready-made reactions and fixations. Can this be prevented in these schools? This does not mean that one must have an open mind. Generally the open mind is like a sieve retaining little or nothing. It is a mind that is capable of quick perception and action that is necessary. That is why we went into the subject of insight with its immediacy of action. Insight does not leave the scar of memory. Generally, experience, as it is understood, leaves its residue as memory, and from this residue one acts. The action strengthens the residue, and so action becomes mechanical. Insight is not a mechanical activity.

Without strengthening the residue that is memory, can it be taught in the school that daily life is a constant process of learning and action in relationship? With most of us the scar of residue becomes all-important, and we lose the swift current of life.

Both the student and the educator live in a state of confusion and disorder outwardly and inwardly. One may not be aware of this fact; if one is, one quickly puts order into outward things, but one is rarely aware of inner confusion and disorder.

God is disorder. Consider the innumerable gods that man has invented, or the one God, the one Saviour, and observe the confusion this has created in the world, the wars it has brought about, the innumerable divisions, the separating beliefs, symbols and images. Isn't this confusion and disorder? We have become accustomed to this; we accept it readily, for our life is so wearisome with boredom and pain that we seek comfort in the gods that thought has conjured up. This has been our way of life for thousands of years. Every civilization has invented gods, and they have been the source of great tyranny, wars and destruction. Their buildings may be extraordinarily beautiful, but inside there is darkness and the source of confusion.

Can one put aside these gods? One must if one is to consider why the human mind accepts disorder politically, religiously and economically and lives in it. What is the source of this disorder – the actuality of it, not the theological reason? Can one put aside the concepts of disorder and be free to inquire into the actual daily source of our disorder – not into what order is but disorder? We can find out what absolute order is only when we have thoroughly investigated disorder and its source. We are so eager to find out what order is, so impatient with disorder, that we are apt to suppress it, thinking thereby to bring about order. Here we are asking not only if there can be absolute order in our daily life, but also whether confusion can end. So our first concern is with disorder and its source. Is it thought? Is it contradictory desires? Is it fear and the search for security? Is it the constant demand for pleasure? Is thought one of the sources or the main reason for the disorder?

It is not merely the writer but you asking these questions. Please bear this in mind all the time. You must discover the source, not be told the source and then repeat that.

Thought, as we have pointed out, is finite, limited; and whatever is limited, however wide its activities may be, inevitably brings confusion. That which is limited is divisive and therefore destructive and confusing. We have gone sufficiently into the nature and structure of thought. To have an insight into the nature of thought is to give it its right place so that it loses its overpowering domination.

Is desire and the changing objects of desire one of the causes of our disorder? To suppress desire is to suppress all sensation, which is to paralyse the mind. We think this is the easy and quick way to end desire, but one cannot suppress it; it is much too strong, much too subtle. You cannot grasp it in your hand and twist it according to your wish, which is another desire. We have talked about desire in a previous letter. Desire can never be suppressed or transmuted or corrupted as right and wrong desire; whatever you do about it, it remains always sensation and desire. Desire for enlightenment and desire for money are the same, though the objects vary.

Can one live without desire? Or to put it differently, can the senses be supremely active without desire coming in? There are both psychological and physical sensory activities. The body seeks warmth, food, sex; there is physical pain and so on. These sensations are natural, but when they enter into the psychological field, the trouble begins. Therein lies our confusion. It is important to understand this, especially when we are young, and to observe the physical sensations without suppression or exaggeration; to be alert, watchful that they do not seep into the psychological inner realm where they do not belong.

That is our difficulty; the whole process happens so quickly because we do not see this, have not understood it, have never really examined what actually takes place. There is immediate sensory response to challenge. This response is natural and is not under the domination of thought, of desire. Our difficulty begins when these sensory responses enter into the psychological realm. The challenge may be a woman or a man, or something pleasant, appetizing, or a lovely garden. The response to this is sensation, and when this sensation enters the psychological field, desire begins and thought with its images seeks the fulfilment of desire.

Our question is how to prevent the natural physical responses from entering into the psychological. Is this possible? It is possible only when you observe the nature of the challenge with great attention and carefully watch your responses. This total attention will prevent the physical responses from entering into the inner psyche.

We are concerned with desire and the understanding of it, not the brutalizing factor of suppressing, avoiding or sublimating. You cannot live without desire. When you are hungry you need food. But to understand, which is to investigate the whole activity of desire, is to give it its right place. Then it will not be a source of disorder in our daily life.

18. INTEGRITY

When there is no measurement,
there is the quality of wholeness

What man has done to man has no limit. He has tortured him; he has burnt him; he has killed him; he has exploited him in every possible way – religious, political and economic. This has been the story of man against man; the clever exploit the stupid, the ignorant. All philosophies are intellectual and therefore not whole. These philosophies have enslaved man. They have invented concepts of what society should be and sacrificed man to their concepts; the ideals of the so-called thinkers have dehumanised man. Exploitation of another man or woman seems to be the way of our daily life. We use each other, and each one accepts this. Out of this peculiar relationship, dependence arises with all the misery, confusion and agony that is inherent in dependence. Man has been both inwardly and outwardly so treacherous to himself and to others. How can there be love in these circumstances?

So it becomes very important for the educator to feel total responsibility in his personal relationship not only to the student but to the whole of mankind. He is mankind. If he does not feel responsible for himself totally, then he will be incapable of feeling the passion of total responsibility which is love. Do you as an educator feel this responsibility? If not, why not? You may feel responsible for your own wife, husband or children, and may disregard or feel no responsibility for another, but if you feel completely responsible in yourself, you cannot but be responsible for the whole of humanity.

The question of why you do not feel responsible for another is very important. Responsibility is not an emotional reaction, not something you impose upon yourself – to feel responsible. Then it becomes duty, and duty has lost the perfume or the beauty of the inward quality of total responsibility. It is not something you invite as a principle or an idea to hold on to, like possessing a chair or a watch. A mother may feel responsible for her child, feel that the child is part of her blood and flesh, and so give all her care and attention to that baby for some years. Is this maternal instinct responsibility? It may be that we have inherited this peculiar attachment to the child from the first animals. It exists in all nature from the tiniest bird to the majestic elephant. We are asking if this instinct is responsibility. If it were, parents would feel responsible for a right kind of education, for a totally different kind of society. They would see that there were no wars and that they themselves flowered in goodness.

So it appears that a human being is not concerned for another but is committed only to himself. This commitment is total irresponsibility. His own emotions, his own personal desires, his own attachments, his success, his advancement will inevitably breed ruthlessness both open and subtle. Is this the way of true responsibility?

In these schools the one who gives and the one who receives are both responsible, so they can never indulge in the peculiar quality of separateness. Egotistic separateness is perhaps the very root of the degeneration of the wholeness of the mind with which we are deeply concerned. This does not mean that there is no personal relationship, with affection, with tenderness, with encouragement and support; but when personal relationship becomes all-important and is responsible only for the few, then the mischief has begun. The reality of this is known to every human being. This fragmentation of relationship is the degenerating factor in our lives. We have broken up relationship so that it is to the personal, to a group, to a nation, to certain concepts, and so on.

That which is fragmented can never comprehend the wholeness of responsibility. From the little we are always trying to capture the greater. The better is not the good, and all our thought is based on the better, the more – being better at exams, having better jobs, greater status, better gods, nobler ideas. The better is the outcome of comparison. The thought of the better picture, the better technique, the greater musician, the more talented, the more beautiful and the more intelligent depend on this comparison. We rarely look at a painting for itself, or at a man or a woman for themselves. There is always this quality of comparison.

Is love comparison? Can you ever say you love this one more than that one? When there is this comparison, is that love? When there is this feeling of the more, which is measurement, then thought is in operation. Love is not the movement of thought. This measurement is comparison. We are encouraged throughout our life to compare. When in your school you compare B with A, you are destroying both of them. So is it possible to educate without any sense of comparison?

Why do we compare? We compare for the simple reason that measuring is the way of thought and the way of our life. We are educated in this corruption. The better is always nobler than what is, than what is actually going on. The observation of what is, without comparison, without the measure, is to go beyond what is.

When there is no comparison, there is integrity. It is not that you are true to yourself, which is a form of measurement, but when there is no measurement at all there is the quality of wholeness. The essence of the ego, the "me", is measurement. When there is measurement, there is fragmentation. This must be profoundly understood, not as an idea but as an actuality. When you read this statement, you may make an abstraction of it as an idea, a concept, and the abstraction is another form of measurement. That which is has no measurement.

Please give your heart to the understanding of this. When you have grasped the full significance of this, your relationship with the student and with your own family will become something quite different. If you ask if that difference will be better, then you are caught in the wheel of measurement. Then you are lost. You will find the difference when you actually test this out. The very word difference implies measurement, but we are using the word non-comparatively. Almost every word we use has this feeling of measurement, so the words affect our reactions, and reactions deepen the sense of comparison. The word and the reaction are interrelated, and the art lies in not being conditioned by the word, which means that language does not shape us. Use the word without the psychological reactions to it.

As we have said, we are concerned with communicating with each other about the nature of the degeneration of our minds and so the ways of our life. Enthusiasm is not passion. You can be enthusiastic about something one day and lose it the next. You can be enthusiastic about playing football and lose interest when it no longer entertains you. But passion is something entirely different. It has no time-lag in it.

19. PROBLEMS

Physical and psychological problems
waste our energy

As a rule, parents have very little time for their children except when they are babies. They send them to the local or boarding schools, or they allow others to look after them. They may not have time or the necessary patience to educate them at home. They are occupied with their own problems. So our schools become the children's homes and the educators become the parents with all the responsibility. We have written about this earlier, and it is not out of place to repeat it: home is a place where there is a certain freedom, a sense of being secure, being provided for and sheltered. Do the children in these schools feel that they are being carefully watched over, given a great deal of thought and affection, and that there is concern for their behaviour, their food, their clothes and their manners? If so, the school becomes a place where the student feels that he is really at home, with all its implications, that there are people around him who are looking after his tastes, the way he talks; that he is being looked after physically as well as psychologically, being helped to be free from hurts and fear. This is the responsibility of every teacher in these schools, not of one or two. The whole school exists for this, for an atmosphere in which both the educators and the students are flowering in goodness.

The educator needs leisure to be quiet by himself, to gather the energy that has been expended, to be aware of his own personal problems and resolve them, so that when he meets the students again he does not carry the noise of his personal turmoil. As we have pointed out earlier, any problem arising in our lives should be resolved instantly or as quickly as possible, for when problems are carried from day to day, the sensitivity of the whole mind degenerates. This sensitivity is essential. We lose this sensitivity when we are merely instructing the student in a subject. When the subject becomes the only important thing, sensitivity fades away, and then you really lose contact with the student. The student then is merely a receptacle for information. Thus your mind and the student's mind become mechanical.

Generally, we are sensitive to our own problems, to our own desires and thoughts, and rarely to those of others. When we are constantly in contact with the students, there is a tendency to impose our own images on them or, if the student has his own strong images, there is conflict between these images. So it becomes very important that the educator should leave his images at home and be concerned with the images that parents or society have imposed on the student, or the images that the student himself has created.

Physical and psychological problems waste our energy. Can the educator be physically secure in these schools and be free of psychological problems? This is really important to understand. When there is not a sense of physical security, uncertainty brings about psychological turmoil. This encourages dullness of the mind, so the passion that is so necessary in our daily life withers away and enthusiasm takes its place. Enthusiasm is a dangerous thing for it is never constant. It rises in a wave and is gone. This is mistaken for seriousness. You may be enthusiastic, eager, active for some time about what you are doing, but inherent in it is dissipation. Again it is essential that we understand this, for most relationship is prone to this waste.

Passion is wholly different from lust, interest or enthusiasm. Interest in something can be very deep and you can use that interest for profit or for power, but that interest is not passion. Interest may be stimulated by an object or by an idea. Interest is self-indulgence. Passion is free of the self. Enthusiasm is always about something. Passion is a flame in itself. Enthusiasm can be aroused by another, something outside of you. Passion is the summation of energy, which is not the outcome of any kind of stimulation. Passion is beyond the self.

Do the teachers have this sense of passion? For out of this comes creation. In teaching subjects, one has to find new ways of transmitting information without the information making the mind mechanical. Can you teach history, which is the story of mankind, not as Indian, English, American history, but as the story of mankind, which is global? Then the educator's mind is always fresh, eager, discovering a whole different approach to teaching. In this the educator is intensely alive, and with this aliveness goes passion.

Can this be done in all our schools? For we are concerned with bringing about a different society, with the flowering of goodness, with a non-mechanical mind. True education is this. Will you, the educators, undertake this responsibility? In this responsibility lies the flowering of goodness in you and in the student. We are responsible for the whole of mankind, which is you and the student. You have to start there and cover the whole earth. You can go very far if you start very near. The nearest is you and your student. We generally start with the farthest, the supreme principle, the greatest ideal, and get lost in some hazy dream of imaginative thought. But when you start very near, with the nearest, which is you, then the whole world is open, for you are the world, and the world beyond you is only nature. Nature is not imaginary, it is actual; and what is happening to you now is actual. You must begin from the actual, with what is happening now. And the now is timeless.

20. STATUS

Selfishness is the essential problem
of our life

Most human beings are selfish. They are not conscious of their own selfishness, it is the way of their life. And if one is aware that one is selfish, one hides it very carefully and conforms to the pattern of society, which is essentially selfish. The selfish mind is very cunning. Either it is brutally and openly selfish, or it takes many forms. If you are a politician, the selfishness seeks power, status and popularity; it identifies itself with an idea, a mission, all for the public good. If you are a tyrant, it expresses itself in brutal domination. If you are inclined to be religious, it takes the form of adoration, devotion, adherence to some belief, some dogma. It also expresses itself in the family; the father pursues his own selfishness in the ways of his life, and so does the mother.

Fame, prosperity, good looks form a basis for this hidden creeping movement of the self. It is in the hierarchical structure of the priesthood, however much they may proclaim their love of God, their adherence to the self-created image of their particular deity. The captains of industry and the poor clerk have this expanding and benumbing sensuality of the self. The monks who have renounced the ways of the world may wander the face of the world or may be locked away in some monastery, but they have not left this unending movement of the self. They may change their names, put on robes or take vows of celibacy or silence, but they burn with some ideal, with some image, some symbol.

It is the same with the scientists, with the philosophers and the professors in the universities. The doer of good works, the saints and gurus, the man or the woman who works endlessly for the poor, all attempt to lose themselves in their work, but the work is part of the self. They have transferred the egotism to their labours. It begins in childhood and continues to old age. The conceit of knowledge, the practised humility of the leader, the submitting wife and dominating man all have this disease. The self identifies with the State, with endless groups, with endless ideas and causes, but it remains what it was at the beginning.

Human beings have tried various practices, methods, meditations to be free of this centre which causes so much misery and confusion but, like a shadow, it is never captured. It is always there, and it slips through your fingers, through your mind. Sometimes it is strengthened or becomes weak according to circumstances. You corner it here, it turns up there.

One wonders if the educator, who is responsible for a new generation, understands non-verbally what a mischievous thing the self is, how corrupting, distorting, how dangerous it is in our lives. He may not know how to be free of it; he may not even be aware it is there; but once he sees the nature of the movement of the self, can he or she convey its subtleties to the student? Isn't it the teacher's responsibility to do this? Insight into the working of the self is of greater importance than academic learning. Knowledge can be used by the self for its own expansion, its aggressiveness, its innate cruelty.

Selfishness is the essential problem of our life. Conforming and imitation are part of the self, as are competition and the ruthlessness of talent. If the educator in these schools takes this problem to his heart seriously, which I hope he does, then how will he help the student to be selfless? You might say it is a "gift of strange gods", or brush it aside as being impossible; but if you are serious, as one must be, and are totally responsible for the student, how will you set about freeing the mind from this age-old, binding energy, this self which has caused so much sorrow?

Wouldn't you, with great care, which implies affection, explain in simple words what the consequences are when the student speaks in anger, or when he hits somebody, or when he is thinking of his own importance? Is it not possible to explain to him that when he insists, 'This is mine', or boasts, 'I did it', or when he avoids a certain action through fear, he is building a wall, brick by brick, around himself? Is it not possible when his desires, his sensations overpower his rational thinking, to point out that the shadow of self is growing? Is it not possible to say to him that where the self is, in any guise, there is no love?

But the student might ask the educator, 'Have you realized all this or are you just playing with words?' That very question might awaken your own intelligence, and that very intelligence will give you the right feeling and the right words to answer.

As an educator you have no status; you are a human being with all the problems of life, like a student. The moment you speak from status, you are actually destroying human relationship. Status implies power, and when you are seeking this, consciously or unconsciously, you enter a world of cruelty. You have a great responsibility, my friend, and if you take this total responsibility, which is love, then the roots of the self are gone. This is not said as an encouragement or to make you feel that you must do this, but as we are all human beings, representing the whole of mankind, we are totally and wholly responsible, whether we choose to be or not. You may try to evade it, but that very movement is the action of the self. Clarity of perception is freedom from the self.

21. SENSITIVITY

The intelligence of the body
will guard its own well-being

The flowering of goodness is the release of our total energy. It is not the control or suppression of energy but rather the total freedom of this vast energy. It is limited, narrowed down by thought, by the fragmentation of our senses. Thought itself is this energy manipulating itself into a narrow groove, a centre of the self. The flowering of goodness can be only when energy is free. Thought by its very nature has limited this energy, and so the fragmentation of the senses takes place. Hence there are the senses, sensations, desires, and the images that thought creates out of desire. All this is a fragmentation of energy. Can this limited movement be aware of itself? That is, can the senses be aware of themselves? Can desire see itself arising out of the senses, out of the sensation of the image that thought has created; and can thought be aware of itself, of its movement? All this implies: can the whole physical body be aware of itself?

We live by our senses. One of them is usually dominant: the listening, the seeing, the tasting seem to be separate from each other; but is this a fact? Or is it that we have given to one or other a greater importance, or rather that thought has given the greater importance? One may hear great music and delight in it, and yet be insensitive to other things. One may have a sensitive taste and be wholly insensitive to delicate colour. This is fragmentation. When each fragment is aware only of itself, then fragmentation is maintained. In this way energy is broken up. If this is so, as it appears to be, is there a non-fragmentary awareness by all the senses?

Thought is part of the senses. Can the body be aware of itself? Not you being aware of your own body, but the body itself being aware. This is very important to find out. It cannot be taught by another for then it is second-hand information, which thought is imposing on it. You must discover for yourself whether the whole organism, the physical entity, can be aware of itself. You may be aware of the movement of an arm, a leg or the head, and through that movement feel that you are becoming aware of the whole, but what we are asking is: can the body be aware of itself without any movement? This is essential to find out, because thought has imposed its pattern on the body, what it thinks is right exercise, right food, and so on. So there is the domination of thought over the organism; there is consciously or unconsciously a struggle between thought and the organism. In this way thought is destroying the natural intelligence of the body itself.

Does the body, the physical organism, have its own intelligence? It has when all the senses are acting together in harmony so that there is no straining, no emotional or sensory demands of desire. When one is hungry one eats, but usually taste, formed by habit, dictates what one eats. So fragmentation takes place. A healthy body can be brought about only through the harmony of all the senses, which is the intelligence of the body itself. What we are asking is: doesn't disharmony bring about waste of energy? Can the organism's own intelligence, which has been suppressed or destroyed by thought, be awakened?

Remembrance plays havoc with the body. The remembrance of yesterday's pleasure makes thought master of the body. The body then becomes a slave to the master, and intelligence is denied. So there is conflict. This struggle may express itself as laziness, fatigue, indifference, or in neurotic responses. When the body has its own intelligence freed from thought, though thought is part of it, this intelligence will guard its own well-being.

Pleasure dominates our life in its crudest or most educated forms; and pleasure essentially is a remembrance – that which has been, or that which is anticipated. Pleasure is never at the moment. When pleasure is denied, suppressed or blocked, neurotic acts, such as violence and hatred, take place out of this frustration. Then pleasure seeks other forms and outlets; satisfaction and dissatisfaction arise. To be aware of all these physical and psychological activities requires an observation of the whole movement of one's life.

When the body is aware of itself, then we can ask a further and perhaps more difficult question: can thought, which has put together this whole consciousness, be aware of itself? Most of the time thought dominates the body, and so the body loses its vitality, intelligence, its own intrinsic energy, and hence has neurotic reactions. Is the intelligence of the body different from total intelligence, which can come about only when thought, realizing its own limitation, finds its right place?

As we said at the beginning of this letter, the flowering of goodness can take place only when there is the release of total energy. In this release there is no friction. It is only in this supreme undivided intelligence that there is this flowering. This intelligence is not the child of reason. The totality of this intelligence is compassion.

Mankind has tried to release this immense energy through various forms of control, through exhausting discipline, through fasting, through sacrificial denials offered to some supreme principle or god, or through manipulating this energy through various states. All this implies the manipulation of thought towards a desired end. But what we are saying is quite contrary to all this. Can all this be conveyed to the student? It is your responsibility to do so.

22. SELF-CENTREDNESS

Thought is the root
of all our sorrow, all our ugliness

It is the concern of these schools to bring about a new generation of human beings who are free from self-centred action. No other educational centres are concerned with this. It is our responsibility as educators to bring about a mind that has no conflict within itself, and to end the struggle and conflict in the world about us.

Can the mind, which is a complex structure and movement, free itself from the network it has woven? Every intelligent human being asks whether it is possible to end the conflict between man and man. Some have gone into it very deeply, intellectually; others, seeing the hopelessness of it, become bitter, cynical, or look to some outside agency to deliver them from their own chaos and misery. When we ask whether the mind can free itself from the prison it has created, it is not an intellectual or rhetorical question. It is asked in all seriousness; it is a challenge to which you have to respond, not at your convenience or comfort, but according to the depth of that challenge. It cannot be postponed.

A challenge is not asking whether it is possible or not, whether the mind is capable of freeing itself. The challenge, if it is worth anything at all, is immediate and intense. To respond to it you must have that quality of intensity and immediacy, the feeling of it. When there is this intense approach, then the question has great implications. The challenge is demanding the highest excellence from you, not just intellectually but with every faculty of your being. This challenge is not outside you. Please do not externalise it, which is to make a concept of it. You are demanding of yourself the totality of all your energy. That very demand wipes away all control, all contradiction and any opposition within yourself. It implies a total integrity, complete harmony. This is the essence of not being selfish.

The mind with its emotional responses, with all the things that thought has put together, is our consciousness. This consciousness with its content is the consciousness of every human being. It is modified, not entirely similar, different in its nuances and subtleties, but basically the roots of its existence are common to all of us. Scientists and psychologists are examining this consciousness, and the gurus are playing with it for their own ends. The serious ones are examining consciousness as a concept, as a laboratory process; they are examining the responses of the brain, alpha waves and so on, as something outside themselves.

But we are not concerned with the theories, concepts and ideas about consciousness; we are concerned with its activity in our daily life. In understanding these activities, the daily responses, the conflicts, we will have an insight into the nature and structure of our own consciousness. As we pointed out, the basic reality of this consciousness is common to us all. It is not your particular consciousness or mine. We have inherited it, and we are modifying it, changing it here and there, but its basic movement is common to all mankind.

This consciousness is our mind with all its intricacies of thought, the emotions, the sensory responses, the accumulated knowledge, the suffering, the pain, the anxiety, the violence. All that is our consciousness. The brain is ancient and it is conditioned by centuries of evolution, by every kind of experience, increased by more recent accumulations of knowledge. All this is consciousness in action in every moment of our life. It is the relationship between humans with all the pleasures, pains, confusion of contradictory senses and the gratification of desire with its pain. This is the movement of our life. We are asking – and this must be met as a challenge – whether this ancient movement can ever come to an end. For this has become a mechanical activity, a traditional way of life. In the ending there is a beginning, and then only is there neither ending nor beginning.

Consciousness appears to be a very complex affair, but actually it is very simple. Thought has put together all the content of our consciousness, its security, its uncertainty, its hopes and fears, the depression and elation, the ideals, the illusions. Once it is grasped that thought is responsible for the whole content of our consciousness, then the inevitable question arises whether thought can be stopped. Many attempts have been made, religious and mechanical, to end thought. The very demand for the ending of thought is part of the movement of thought. The very search for super-consciousness is still the measure of thought. The gods, the rituals, all the emotional illusions of churches, temples and mosques, with their marvellous architecture, are still the movement of thought. God is put in heaven by thought. Thought has not made nature; that is real. The chair is also real, and it is made by thought; all the things technology has brought about are real. Illusions avoid the actual – that which is taking place now – but illusions become real because we live by them. The dog is not made by thought, but what we wish the dog to be is the movement of thought. Thought is measure. Thought is time. The whole of this is our consciousness. The mind, the brain, the senses are part of it. We are asking if this movement can come to an end.

Thought is the root of all our sorrow, all our ugliness. What we are asking for is the ending of these things that thought has put together; not the ending of thought itself, but the ending of our anxiety, grief, pain, power, violence. With the ending of these, thought finds its rightful, limited place – the everyday knowledge and memory one must have. When the contents of consciousness, which have been put together by thought, are no longer active, then there is vast space and so the release of immense energy which was limited by consciousness. Love is beyond this consciousness.

23. THE ART OF LIVING

Relationship is the art of living

Questioner: If I may ask you in all seriousness, what do you consider to be one of the most important things in life? I have thought about this matter considerably and there are so many things in life that all seem important.

Krishnamurti: Perhaps it is the art of living. We are using the word art in its widest sense. As life is so complex, it is always difficult and confusing to pick one aspect and say it is the most important. The very choice, the differentiating quality, if I may point out, leads to further confusion. If you say this is the most important, then you relegate the other facts of life to a secondary position. Either we take the whole movement of life as one, which is extremely difficult for most people, or we take one fundamental aspect in which all the others may be included. If you agree to this, then we can proceed with our dialogue.

Q: Do you mean to say that one aspect may cover the whole field of life? Is that possible?

K: It is possible. Let us go into it very slowly and hesitantly. First of all, the two of us must investigate and not immediately come to some conclusion, which is generally rather superficial. We are exploring together one facet of life, and in the very understanding of it we may cover the whole field of life. To investigate, we must be free of our prejudices, personal experiences, and predetermined conclusions. Like a good scientist, we must have a mind unclouded by the knowledge that we have already accumulated. We must come to it afresh, without any reaction to what is being observed. This is one of the necessities in this exploration, which is not the exploration of an idea or a series of philosophical concepts, but of our own minds. This is absolutely necessary; otherwise our investigation is coloured by our own fears, hopes and pleasures.

Q: Aren't you asking too much? Is it possible to have such a mind?

K: The very urge to investigate and the intensity of it free the mind from its colouring. As we said, one of the most important things is the art of living. Is there a way of living our daily life that is entirely different from what it normally is? We all know the usual. Is there a way of living without any control, without any conflict, without a disciplinary conformity? How do I find out? I can only find out when my whole mind is facing exactly what is happening now. This means I can find out what it means to live without conflict only when what is happening now can be observed. This observation is not an intellectual or emotional affair, but acute, clear, sharp perception in which there is no duality. There is only the actual and nothing else.

Q: What do you mean by duality in this instance?

K: That there is no opposition or contradiction in what is going on. Duality arises only when there is an escape from what is. This escape creates the opposite, and so conflict arises. There is only the actual and nothing else.

Q: Are you saying that when something which is happening now is perceived, the mind must not come in with associations and reactions?

K: Yes, that is what we mean. The associations and reactions to what is happening are the conditioning of the mind. This conditioning prevents the observation of what is taking place now. What is taking place now is free of time. Time is the evolution of our conditioning; it is man's inheritance, the burden that has no beginning. When there is this passionate observation of what is going on, that which is being observed dissolves into nothingness. An observation of anger that is taking place now reveals the whole nature and structure of violence. This insight is the ending of all violence. It is not replaced by anything else; and therein lies our difficulty, because our whole desire and urge is to find a definite end. In that end there is an illusory sense of security.

Q: There is difficulty for many of us in the observation of anger because emotions and reactions seem inextricably part of that anger. One doesn't feel anger without associations, content.

K: Anger has many stories behind it. It isn't just a solitary event. It has, as you pointed out, a great many associations. These very associations, with their emotions, prevent actual observation. With anger, the content is the anger; the anger is the content; they are not two separate things. The content is the conditioning. In the passionate observation of what is actually going on, that is, the activities of the conditioning, the nature and structure of the conditioning are dissolved.

Q: Are you saying that when an event is taking place there is the immediate, racing current of associations in the mind and that if one instantly sees this starting to happen, that observation instantly stops it and it is gone? Is this what you mean?

K: Yes. It is really simple, so simple that you miss its very simplicity and so its subtlety. What we are saying is that whatever is happening – when you are walking, talking, "meditating" – the event that is taking place is to be observed. When the mind wanders, the very observation of it ends its chatter. So there is no distraction whatsoever at any time.

Q: It seems as if you are saying that the content of thought essentially has no meaning in the art of living.

K: Yes. Remembrance has no place in the art of living. Relationship is the art of living. If there is remembrance in relationship, it is not relationship. Relationship is between human beings, not between their memories. It is these memories that divide, and so there is contention, the opposition of the "you" and the "me". So thought, which is remembrance, has no place whatsoever in relationship. This is the art of living.

Relationship is to all things – to nature, the birds, the rocks, to everything around us and above us, to the clouds, the stars and to the blue sky. All existence is relationship. Without it you cannot live. Because we have corrupted relationship, we live in a society that is degenerating. The art of living can come into being only when thought does not contaminate love. In these schools can the teacher be wholly committed to this art?

24. WORDS

The word prevents actual perception

The greatest art is the art of living, greater than all things that human beings have created by mind or hand, greater than all the scriptures and their gods. It is only through this art of living that a new culture can come into being. It is the responsibility of every teacher, especially in these schools, to bring this about. This art of living can come only out of total freedom.

This freedom is not an ideal, a thing to take place eventually. The first step in freedom is the last step in it. It is the first step that counts, not the last step. What you do now is far more essential than what you do at some future date. Life is what is happening this instant, not an imagined instant, not what thought has conceived. So it is the first step you take now that is important. If that step is in the right direction, then the whole of life is open to you. The right direction is not towards an ideal, a predetermined end. It is inseparable from that which is taking place now. This is not a philosophy, a series of theories. It is exactly what the word philosophy means – the love of truth, the love of life. It is not something that you go to a university to learn. We are learning about the art of living in our daily life.

We live by words, and words become our prison. Words are necessary to communicate, but the word is never the thing. The actual is not the word, but the word becomes all-important when it has taken the place of that which is. You may observe this phenomenon when the description – the symbol we worship, the shadow we follow, the illusion we cling to – has become the reality instead of the thing itself. Words, the language, shape our reactions. Language becomes the compelling force and our minds are shaped and controlled by the word. The words nation, State, God, family, and so on, envelop us with all their associations, and so our minds become slaves to the pressure of words.

Questioner: How is this to be avoided?

Krishnamurti: The word is never the thing. The word wife is never the person; the word door is not the door. The word prevents the actual perception of the thing or person because the word has many associations. These associations, which are actually remembrances, distort not only visual but also psychological observation. Words then become a barrier to the free flow of observation. Take the words Prime Minister and clerk. They describe functions, but the words Prime Minister have tremendous significance of power, status and importance, whereas the word clerk has associations of unimportance, little status and no power. So the word prevents you from looking at both of them as human beings. There is ingrained snobbery in most of us, and to see what words have done to our thinking and to be choicelessly aware of it is to learn the art of observation – to observe without association.

Q: I understand what you say, but the speed of association is so instantaneous that the reaction takes place before one realizes it. Is it possible to prevent this?

K: Isn't this a wrong question? Who is to prevent it? Is it another symbol, another word, another idea? If it is, then one has not seen the whole significance of the enslavement of the mind by words, language. You see, we use words emotionally; it is a form of emotional thinking, apart from the use of technological words, as in numbers, or measures, which are precise. In human relationship and activity, emotions play a great part. Desire, sustained by thought creating the image, is very strong. The image is the word, is the picture, and this follows our pleasure, our desire. So the whole way of our life is shaped by the word and its associations. To see this entire process as a whole is to see the truth of how thought prevents perception.

Q: Are you saying that there is no thinking without words?

K: Yes, more or less. Please bear in mind that we are talking about the art of living, learning about it, not memorizing the words. We are learning, not I teaching and you becoming a silly disciple. You are asking if there is thinking without words. This is a very important question. Our whole thinking is based on memory, and memory is based on words, images, symbols, pictures. All these are words.

Q: But what one remembers is not a word; it is an experience, an emotional event, a picture of a person or a place. The word is a secondary association.

K: We are using words to describe all this. After all, the word is a symbol to indicate that which has happened or is happening, to communicate or to evoke something. Is there thinking without this whole process? Yes, there is, but it should not be called thinking. Thinking implies a continuation of memory, but perception is not the activity of thought; it is really insight into the whole nature and movement of the word, the symbol, the image and their emotional involvements. To see this as a whole is to give the word its right place.

Q: But what does it mean to see the whole? You say this often. What do you mean by it?

K: Thought is divisive because in itself it is limited. To observe wholly implies the non-interference of thought, to observe without the past as knowledge blocking the observation. Then the observer is not, for the observer is the past, the very nature of thought.

Q: Are you asking us to stop thought?

K: Again, if we may point out, that is a wrong question. If thought tells itself to stop thinking, it creates duality and conflict. This is the very divisive process of thought. If you really grasp the truth of this, then thought is in abeyance naturally. Thought then has its own limited place. Thought then will not take over the whole expanse of life, which it is doing now.

Q: Sir, I see what extraordinary attention is needed. Can I really have that attention; am I serious enough to give my whole energy to this?

K: Can energy be divided at all? Energy is expended in earning a livelihood, in having a family, and in being serious enough to grasp what is being said. It is all energy, but thought divides it, and so we expend much energy on living and very little on the other. This art of living is the art in which there is no division. This is the whole of life.

25. INTELLECT

*Learn from the book
of the story of yourself*

Why are we being educated? Perhaps you never ask this question, but if you do, what is your response to it? Many reasons are put forward for the necessity of being educated, arguments that are reasonable, quite necessary and mundane. The usual reply is to get a job, have a successful career, or to become skilful with your hands or with your mind. Great emphasis is laid upon the capacity of the mind to find itself a good, profitable career. If you are not intellectually bright, then the skill of your hands becomes important. Education is necessary, it is said, to sustain society as it is, to conform to a pattern set by the so-called Establishment, traditional or ultra-modern. The educated mind has great capacity to gather information on almost any subject – art, science, and so on. This informed mind is scholastic, professional, philosophical. Such erudition is greatly praised and honoured. This education, if you are studious, clever, swift in your learning, will assure you a bright future, the brightness of it depending on your social and environmental situation. If you are not so bright in this framework of education, you become a labourer, a factory worker, or you have to find a place at the bottom of this very complex society. This is generally the way of our education.

What is education? It is essentially the art of learning, not only from books, but from the whole movement of life. The printed word has become consumingly all-important. You are learning what other people think, their opinions, their values, their judgements and a variety of their innumerable experiences. The library is more important than the man who has the library. He himself is the library, and he assumes that he is learning by constant reading. This accumulation of information, as in a computer, is considered to make an educated, sophisticated mind. Then there are those who do not read at all, who are rather contemptuous of those who do, and are absorbed in their own self-centred experiences and assertive opinions.

Recognizing all this, what is the function of a holistic mind? We mean by the mind all the responses of the senses, the emotions – which are entirely different from love – and the intellectual capacity. We now give fantastic importance to the intellect. We mean by the intellect the capacity to reason logically, sanely or without sanity, objectively or personally. It is the intellect with its movement of thought that brings about fragmentation of our human condition. It is the intellect that has divided the world linguistically, nationally, religiously – divided man from man. The intellect is the central factor of the degeneration of mankind throughout the world, for the intellect is only a part of the human condition and capacity. When the part is extolled, praised and given honours, when it assumes all-importance, then one's life – which is relationship, action, conduct – becomes contradictory, hypocritical. Then anxiety and guilt come into being. Intellect has its place, as in science, but man has used scientific knowledge, not only for his benefit, but to bring about instruments of war and pollution of the earth. The intellect can perceive its own activities, which bring about degeneration, but it is utterly incapable of putting an end to its own decline, because essentially it is only a part.

As we have said, education is the essence of learning. Learning about the nature of the intellect, its dominance, its activities, its vast capacities and its destructive power, is education. To learn the nature of thought, which is the very movement of the intellect, not from a book but from the observation of the world about you, to learn what exactly is happening, without theories, prejudices and values, is education. To learn from books is important, but what is far more important is to learn from the book of the story of yourself, because you are all mankind. To read that book is the art of learning. It is all there – the institutions, their pressures, the religious impositions and doctrines, their cruelty, their faiths. The social structure of all societies is the relationship between human beings with their greed, their ambitions, their violence, their pleasures, their anxieties. It is there if you know how to look.

The book is not out there or hidden in yourself; it is all around you; you are part of that book. The book tells you the story of the human being, and it is to be read in your relationships, in your reactions, in your concepts and values. The book is the very centre of your being, and the learning is to read that book with exquisite care. The book tells you the story of the past, how the past shapes your mind, your heart and your senses. The past shapes the present, modifying itself according to the challenge of the moment. And in this endless movement of time human beings are caught. This is the conditioning of man.

This conditioning has been the endless burden of man, of you and your brother. The philosophers, the theologians, the saints have accepted this conditioning, have allowed the acceptance of it, making the best of it; or they have offered escapes into fantasies of mystical experiences, of gods and heavens. Education is the art of learning about this conditioning and the way out of it, the freedom from this burden. There is a way out, which is not an escape, which does not accept things as they are. It is not the avoidance of the conditioning; it is not the suppression of it. It is the dissolution of the conditioning.

When you read this or when you hear it, be aware of whether you are listening or reading with the verbal capacity of the intellect, or with the care of attention. When there is total attention, there is no past but only the pure observation of what is actually going on.

26. VIOLENCE

Comparison
is one of the many aspects of violence

One is apt to forget or disregard the responsibility of the educator to bring about a new generation of human beings who are psychologically, inwardly, free of miseries, anxieties and travail. It is a sacred responsibility, not to be easily set aside for one's own ambitions, status or power. If the educator feels such a responsibility – the greatness of it and the depth and beauty of that responsibility – he will find the capacity to instruct and to sustain his own energy.

This demands great diligence, not a periodic, haphazard endeavour. The very profound responsibility will kindle the fire that will maintain the educator as a total human being and a great teacher. As the world is rapidly degenerating, there must be in all these schools a group of teachers and students who are dedicated to bringing about a radical transformation of human beings through right education. The word right is not a matter of opinion, evaluation or some concept invented by the intellect. The word right denotes total action in which all self-interested motive ceases. The very dominant responsibility, the concern not only of the educator but also of the student, banishes self-perpetuating problems. However immature the mind, once you accept this responsibility that very acceptance brings about the flowering of the mind. This flowering is in the relationship between the student and the educator. It is not a one-sided affair.

When you read this, please give your total attention and feel the urgency and intensity of this responsibility. Please do not make it into an abstraction, an idea, but rather observe the actual fact, the actual happening in the reading of this.

Almost all human beings in their lives desire power and wealth. When there is wealth, there is a sense of freedom, and pleasure is pursued. The desire for power seems to be an instinct which expresses itself in many ways. It is in the priest, the guru, the husband or the wife or in the action of one student towards another. The desire to dominate or to submit is one of the conditions of mankind, probably inherited from the animal. This aggressiveness and the yielding to it pervert all relationships throughout life. This has been the pattern from the beginning of time. Humanity has accepted this as a natural way of life, with all the conflicts and miseries it brings.

Basically, measurement is involved in it – the more and the less, the greater and the smaller – which is essentially comparison. One is always comparing oneself with another, comparing one painting with another. There is comparison between the greater power and the lesser, between the timid and the aggressive. This constant measurement of power, position, wealth begins almost at birth and continues throughout life. This is encouraged in schools, colleges and universities. Their whole system of gradation is this giving comparative value to knowledge. When A is compared to B who is clever, bright, assertive, that very comparison destroys A. This destruction takes the form of competition, of imitation of and conformity to the patterns set by B. This breeds, consciously or unconsciously, antagonism, jealousy, anxiety and even fear; and this becomes the condition in which A lives for the rest of his life, always measuring, always comparing psychologically and physically.

This comparison is one of the many aspects of violence. The word more is always comparative, as is the word better. The question is: can the educator put aside all comparison, all measurement, in his teaching? Can he take the student as he is, not as what he should be, and not make judgements based on comparative evaluations? It is only when there is comparison between the one called clever and the one called dull that there is such a quality as dullness.

Is an idiot so because of comparison, or because he is incapable of certain activities? We set certain standards which are based on measurement, and those who do not come up to them are considered deficient. When the educator puts aside comparison and measurement, then he is concerned with the student as he is, and his relationship with the student is direct and totally different. This is really very important to understand. Love is not comparative. It has no measurement.

Comparison and measurement are ways of the intellect. This is divisive. When this is understood basically, not the verbal meaning but the actual truth of it, the relationship of teacher and student undergoes a radical change. The ultimate tests of measurement are examinations accompanied by fear and anxieties, which deeply affect the future life of the student. The whole atmosphere of a school undergoes a change when there is no sense of competition, comparison.

27. VALUES

Live with clarity, which is not a value

It is one of the peculiarities of human beings to cultivate values. From childhood, we are encouraged to set certain deep-rooted values for ourselves. Each person has his own long-lasting purposes and intents and naturally the values of one differ from those of another. These are cultivated either by desire or by the intellect. They are either illusory, comfortable, consoling, or factual. These values obviously encourage division between human beings. Values are ignoble or noble according to one's prejudices and intentions.

We can ask, without listing various types of values, why it is that human beings have values and what their consequences are. The root meaning of the word value is strength. It comes from the word valour. Strength is not a value. It becomes a value when it is the opposite of weakness. Strength – not strength of character, which is the result of the pressure of society – is the essence of clarity. Clear thinking is without prejudices, without bias; it is observation without distortion. Strength or valour is not a thing to be cultivated as you would cultivate a plant or a new breed. It is not a result. A result has a cause, and when there is a cause it indicates a weakness. The consequences of weakness are resistance or yielding. Clarity has no cause. Clarity is not an effect or result; it is the pure observation of thought and thought's total activity. This clarity is strength.

So why have human beings projected values? Is it to give guidance in daily life? Is it to give them a sense of purpose without which life seems uncertain, vague, without direction? But the direction is set by the intellect or desire, and so the very direction becomes a distortion. These distortions vary from man to man, and man clings to them in the restless ocean of confusion. One can observe the consequences of having values: they separate one human being from another and set them against one another. Extended, this leads to misery, to violence and ultimately to war.

Ideals are values. Ideals of any kind are a series of values – national, religious, collective, or personal – and one can observe the consequences of these ideals as they are taking place in the world. When one sees the truth of this, the mind is freed of all values. For such a mind there is only clarity. A mind that clings to or desires an experience is pursuing the fallacy of value, and so becomes private, secretive and divisive.

As an educator, can you explain to a student the need to have no values whatsoever, but to live with clarity which is not a value? This can be brought about when the educator himself has felt deeply the truth of this. If he has not, then it becomes merely a verbal explanation without any deep significance. This has to be conveyed not only to the older students but also to the very young. The older students are already heavily conditioned through the pressure of society and of parents with their values; or they themselves have projected their own goals which become their prison. With the very young, what is most important is to help them to free themselves from psychological pressures and problems. The very young are now being taught complicated intellectual problems; their studies are becoming more and more technical; they are given more and more abstract information; various forms of knowledge are being imposed on their brains, thus conditioning them right from childhood.

What we are concerned with is to help the very young to have no psychological problems, to be free of fear, anxiety, cruelty, and to have care, generosity and affection. This is far more important than the imposition of knowledge on their young minds. This does not mean that the child should not learn to read, write and so on, but the emphasis is on psychological freedom instead of the acquisition of knowledge, though that is necessary. This freedom does not mean the child doing what he wants to do, but understanding the nature of his reactions and his desires.

This requires a great deal of insight on the part of the teacher. After all, you want the student to be a complete human being without any psychological problems; otherwise he will misuse any knowledge he is given. Our education is to live in the known and so be a slave to the past with all its traditions, memories, experiences. Our life is from the known to the known, so there is never freedom from the known. If one lives constantly in the known, there is nothing new, nothing original, nothing uncontaminated by thought. Thought is the known. If our education is the constant accumulation of the known, then our minds and hearts become mechanical, without that immense vitality of the unknown. That which has continuity as knowledge is everlastingly limited; and that which is limited must everlastingly create problems. The ending of continuity, which is time, is the flowering of the timeless.

28. CENTRES OF LEARNING

*These places exist
for the enlightenment of humanity*

Teachers or educators are human beings. Their function is to help the student to learn not only this or that subject, but to understand the whole activity of learning; not only to gather information about various subjects, but primarily to be complete human beings. These schools are not merely centres of learning, they must be centres of goodness and bring about a religious mind.

All over the world, human beings are degenerating to a greater or lesser extent. When pleasure, personal or collective, becomes the dominant interest in life – the pleasure of sex, the pleasure of asserting one's own will, the pleasure of excitement, the pleasure of self-interest, the pleasure of power and status, the insistent demand to have one's own pleasure fulfilled – there is degeneration. When human relationships become casual, based on pleasure, there is degeneration. When responsibility has totally lost its meaning, when there is no care for another or for the earth and the things of the sea, this disregard of heaven and earth is another form of degeneration. When there is hypocrisy in high places, when there is dishonesty in commerce, when lies are part of everyday speech, when there is the tyranny of the few, when only things predominate, there is the betrayal of all life. Then killing becomes the only language of life. When love is taken as pleasure, then human beings have cut themselves off from beauty and the sacredness of life.

Pleasure is always personal, an isolating process. Though one thinks pleasure is something shared with another through gratification, it is actually an enclosing, isolating action of the ego, of the "me". The greater the pleasure, the greater is the strengthening of the "me". When there is pursuit of pleasure, human beings are exploiting each other. When pleasure becomes dominant in our lives, relationship is exploited for this purpose, and so there is no actual relationship with another. Then relationship becomes merchandise.

The urge for fulfilment is based on pleasure, and when that pleasure is denied or has not found means of expression, then there is anger, cynicism, hatred or bitterness. This incessant pursuit of pleasure is actually insanity.

All this indicates, doesn't it, that man, in spite of his vast knowledge and extraordinary capacities, his driving energy and aggressive action, is on the decline? This calculated self-centredness with its fears, pleasures and anxieties is evident throughout the world.

What, then, is the total responsibility of these schools? Surely they must be centres for learning a way of life that is not based on pleasure, on self-centred activities, but on the understanding of correct action, the depth and beauty of relationship, and the sacredness of a religious life. When the world around us is so utterly destructive and without meaning, these schools, these centres, must become places of light and wisdom. It is the responsibility of those who are in charge of these places to bring this about.

As this is urgent, excuses have no meaning. Either the centres are like a rock round which the waters of destruction flow, or they go with the current of decay. These places exist for the enlightenment of humanity.

29. HUMAN SURVIVAL

The desire to be separate
is the source of destruction

In a world where mankind feels threatened by social upheavals, overpopulation, wars, terrifying violence and callousness, each human being is more than ever concerned with his own survival. Survival implies living sanely, happily, without great pressure or strain. Each one of us translates survival according to his own particular concept. The idealist projects a way of life that is not the actual; the theoreticians, whether Marxist, religious, or of any other particular persuasion, have laid down patterns for survival; the nationalists consider survival possible only in a particular group or community. These ideological differences, ideals and faiths are the roots of a division that is preventing human survival.

Human beings want to survive in particular ways, according to their narrow responses, according to their immediate pleasures, according to some faith, according to some religious saviour, prophet or saint. All these cannot bring security; in themselves they are divisive, exclusive, limited. To live in the hope of survival according to a tradition, however ancient or modern, has no meaning. Partial solutions of any kind, whether they are scientific, religious, political, or economic, can no longer assure mankind's survival. Man has been concerned with his own individual survival, with his family, with his group, his tribal nation; and because all this is divisive it threatens his actual survival.

The modern divisions of nationalities, of colour, of culture, of religion are the causes of man's uncertainty about survival. In the turmoil of today's world, uncertainty has made man turn to authorities, to the political, religious or economic experts. The specialist is inevitably a danger because his response must always be partial, limited. Man is no longer individual, separate. What affects the few affects all mankind. There is no escape or avoidance of the problem; you can no longer withdraw from the totality of the human predicament.

We have stated the problem, the cause, and now we must find the solution. This solution must not depend on any kind of pressure – sociological, religious, economic, political, or from any organization. We cannot possibly survive if we are concerned only with our own survival. All human beings the world over are interrelated today. What happens in one country affects the others. Man has considered himself an individual separate from others, but psychologically a human being is inseparable from the whole of mankind.

There is no such thing as psychological survival. When there is the desire to survive or to fulfil, you are psychologically creating a situation which not only separates, but which is totally unreal. Psychologically, you cannot be separate from another. The desire to be separate psychologically is the very source of danger and destruction. Each person by asserting himself threatens his own existence. When the truth of this is seen and understood, man's responsibility undergoes a radical change, not only towards his immediate environment, but towards all living things. This total responsibility is compassion. This compassion acts through intelligence. This intelligence is not partial, individual, separate. Compassion is never partial. Compassion is for the sacredness of all living things.

30. COOPERATION

Cooperation demands great honesty

We ought to consider very seriously, not only in these schools but also as human beings, the capacity to work together – to work together with nature, the living things of the earth, and also with other human beings. As social beings, we exist for ourselves. Our laws, our governments, our religions all emphasize the separateness of humanity, and during the centuries this has developed into man against man. It is becoming more and more important, if we are to survive, that there be a spirit of cooperation with the universe, with all the things of the sea and earth.

One can see in all social structures the destructive effect of fragmentation taking place: nation against nation, one group against another group, one family against another family, one individual against another. It is the same religiously, socially and economically. Each one is striving for himself, for his class, or his particular interest in the community. This division of beliefs, ideals, conclusions and prejudices is preventing the spirit of cooperation from flowering.

We are human beings, not tribal identities, exclusive and separate. We are human beings caught in conclusions, theories, faiths. We are living creatures, not labels. It is our human circumstance that makes us search for food, clothes and shelter at the expense of others. Our very thinking is separative, and all action springing from this limited thought must prevent cooperation. The economic and social structure, as it is now, including organized religions, intensifies exclusiveness, separateness. This lack of cooperation ultimately brings about wars and the destruction of man. It is only during crises or disasters that we seem to come together, and when they are over we are back to our old condition.

We seem to be incapable of living and working together harmoniously. Has this isolating, aggressive process come about because our brain, which is the centre of our thought, our feeling, has from ancient days become through necessity so conditioned to seek its own personal survival? Is it because this isolating process identifies itself with the family, with the tribe, and becomes glorified nationalism? Isn't all isolation linked to a need for identification and fulfilment? Hasn't the importance of the self been cultivated through evolution by the opposition of the "me" and the "you", the "we" and the "they"? Haven't all religions emphasized personal salvation, personal enlightenment, personal achievement, both religiously and in the world? Has cooperation become impossible because we have given such importance to talent, to specialization, to achievement, to success, which all emphasize separateness? Is it because human cooperation has centred on some kind of authority of government or religion, around some ideology or conclusion, which then inevitably brings about its own destructive opposite?

What does it mean to cooperate, not the word but the spirit of it? You cannot possibly cooperate with another, with the earth and its waters, unless you in yourself are harmonious, not broken up, not contradictory. You cannot cooperate if you yourself are under strain, pressure, conflict. How can you cooperate with the universe if you are concerned with yourself, your problems, your ambitions? There can be no cooperation if all your activities are self-centred and you are occupied with your own selfishness, with your own secret desires and pleasures. As long as the intellect with its thoughts dominates all your actions, obviously there can be no cooperation, for thought is partial, narrow and everlastingly divisive. Cooperation demands great honesty.

Honesty has no motive. Honesty is not some ideal, some faith. Honesty is clarity, the clear perception of things as they are. Perception is attention. That very attention throws light, with all its energy, on that which is being observed. This light of perception brings about a transformation of the thing observed.

There is no system through which you learn to cooperate. It is not to be structured and classified. Its very nature demands that there be love, and that love is not measurable; for when you compare, which is the essence or measurement, thought has entered. Where thought is, love is not.

Now, can this be conveyed to the student, and can cooperation exist among educators in these schools? These schools are centres of a new generation with a new outlook, with a new sense of being citizens of the world, concerned with all the living things of this world. It is your grave responsibility to bring about this spirit of co-operation.

31. INTELLIGENCE

*The very nature of intelligence
is sensitivity, which is love*

Intelligence and the capacity of the intellect are two entirely different things. Perhaps these two words derive from the same root, but in order to clarify the full significance of compassion we must be able to distinguish the difference in meaning between the two. Intellect is the capacity to discern, to reason, imagine, to create illusions, to think clearly and also to think non-objectively, personally. Intellect is generally considered different from emotion, but we use the word intellect to convey the whole human capacity for thought. Thought is the response of memory accumulated through various experiences, real or imagined, which are stored as knowledge in the brain. So the capacity of the intellect is to think. Thinking is limited under all circumstances, and when the intellect dominates our activities in both the outer and inner world, naturally our actions must be partial, incomplete. This brings about regret, anxiety and pain.

All theories and ideologies are in themselves partial, and when scientists, technicians and so-called philosophers dominate our society, our morals, and so our daily lives, then we are never faced with the realities of what is actually going on. These influences colour our perceptions, our direct understanding. It is the intellect that finds explanations for wrong-doing as well as for right-doing. It rationalizes misbehaviour, killing and wars. It defines the good as the opposite of the bad. The good has no opposite. If the good were related to the bad, then goodness would have in it the seeds of the bad. Then it would not be goodness. But the intellect is incapable, because of its own divisive capacity, to understand the fullness of the good.

The intellect, thought, is always comparing, evaluating, competing, imitating; so we become conforming, second-hand human beings. The intellect has given enormous benefits to mankind, but it has also brought about great destruction. It has cultivated the arts of war, but it is incapable of wiping away the barriers between human beings. Anxiety is part of the nature of the intellect, as is hurt, for the intellect, which is thought, creates the image which is then capable of being hurt.

When one understands the whole nature and movement of the intellect and thought, one can begin to investigate what intelligence is. Intelligence is the capacity to perceive the whole. Intelligence is incapable of dividing the senses, the emotions and the intellect from each other; it regards them as one unitary movement. Because its perception is always whole, intelligence is incapable of dividing man from man and of setting man against nature. Because in its very nature intelligence is whole, it is incapable of killing.

Practically all religions have said do not kill, but they have never prevented killing. Some religions have said that the things of the earth, including the living creatures, are put there for man's use – therefore kill and destroy them. Killing for pleasure, killing for commerce, killing for nationalism, killing for ideologies, killing for one's faith are all accepted as a way of life. As we are killing the living things of the earth and of the sea we are becoming more and more isolated, and in this isolation we become more and more greedy, seeking pleasure in every form. Intellect may perceive this, but it is incapable of complete action. Intelligence, which is inseparable from love, will never kill. "Not to kill", if it is a concept, an ideal, is not intelligence.

When intelligence is active in our daily life it will tell us when to cooperate and when not to. The very nature of intelligence is sensitivity, and this sensitivity is love. Without this intelligence there can be no compassion. Compassion is not the doing of charitable acts or social reform; it is free from sentiment, romanticism and emotional enthusiasm. It is as strong as death. It is like a great rock, immovable in the midst of confusion, misery and anxiety. Without this compassion no new culture or society can come into being.

Compassion and intelligence walk together; they are not separate. Compassion acts through intelligence. It can never act through the intellect. Compassion is the essence of the wholeness of life.

105

32. THE MOVEMENT OF THOUGHT

Thought uses and destroys

Human beings throughout the world have made the intellect one of the most important factors in our daily life. The ancient Hindus, the Egyptians and the Greeks have all considered intellect the most important function in life. Even the Buddhists have given importance to it. In every university, college and school throughout the world, whether under totalitarian regimes or in so-called democracies, intellect has played a dominant role.

We mean by the intellect the capacity to understand, to discern, to choose, to weigh – as in all the technology of modern science. Isn't the essence of the intellect the whole movement of thought? Thought dominates the world in both the outer life and the inner life. Thought has created all the gods of the world, all the rituals, the dogmas, the beliefs. Thought has also created the cathedrals, the temples, the mosques, with their marvellous architecture, and the local shrines. Thought has been responsible for the never-ending and expansive technology, the wars and the material of wars, the division of people into nations, into classes and into races. Thought has been, and probably still is, the instigator of torture in the name of God, of peace, of order. It has also been responsible for revolution, for the terrorists, for [conceiving an] ultimate principle and pragmatic ideals. By thought we live. Our actions are based on thought; our relationships are also founded on thought. So intellect has been worshipped throughout the ages.

But thought has not created nature – the heavens with their expanding stars, the earth with all its beauty, with its vast seas and green lands. Thought has not created the tree, but thought has used the tree to build the house, to make the chair. Thought uses and destroys.

Thought cannot create love, affection and the quality of beauty. It has woven a network of illusions and actualities. When we live by thought alone, with all its complexities and subtleties, with its purposes and directions, we lose the great depth of life, for thought is superficial. Though it pretends to delve deeply, the very instrument is incapable of penetrating beyond its own limitations. It can project the future, but that future is born of the roots of the past. The things which thought has created are actual, real – like a table, like the image you worship. The image, the symbol that you worship and many romantic, idealistic, humanitarian illusions are put together by thought. Human beings accept and live with the things of thought – money, position, status and the luxury of a freedom that money brings. This is the whole movement of thought and the intellect, and through this narrow window of our life we look at the world.

Is there any movement that is not of the intellect and thought? This has been the inquiry of many religious, philosophical and scientific endeavours. When we use the word religion, we do not mean the nonsense of belief, rituals, dogma and hierarchical structure. We mean by religious men or religious women those who have freed themselves from centuries of propaganda, from the dead weight of tradition, ancient or modern. The philosophers who indulge in theories, in concepts, in ideational pursuits cannot possibly explore beyond the narrow window of thought, nor will the scientist with his extraordinary capacities, with his perhaps original thinking, with his immense knowledge. Knowledge is the storehouse of memory, but there must be freedom from the known to explore that which is beyond it. For that there must be freedom to inquire without any bondage, without any attachment to one's experience, to one's conclusions, to all the things man has imposed upon himself. For that exploration, the intellect must be still in absolute quietness without a murmur of thought.

Our education now is based on the cultivation of the intellect, of thought and knowledge, which are necessary in the field of our daily action; but they have no place in our psychological relationship with each other, for the very nature of thought is divisive and destructive. When thought dominates all our activities and all our relationships, it brings about a world of violence, terror, conflict and misery.

In these schools the dominance of thought must be a concern of all of us, the young and the old.

33. KNOWING YOURSELF

*You have to be good
because you are the future*

We ought to understand right from the beginning of this new year that we are primarily concerned with the psychological aspect of our life, though we are not going to neglect the physical, biological side. What one is inwardly will eventually bring about a good society or the gradual deterioration of human relationship. We are concerned with both aspects of life, not giving one or the other predominance, although the psychological – that is, what we are inwardly – will dictate our behaviour, our relationship with others.

We seem to neglect wholly the deeper and wider realities of life, and give far greater importance to physical aspects, to everyday activities, however relevant or irrelevant. So please bear in mind that in these letters we are approaching our existence from the inner to the outer, not the other way round. Though most people are concerned with the outer, our education must be concerned with bringing about a harmony between the outer and inner; this cannot possibly come about if our eyes are fixed only on the outer.

We mean by the inner all the movement of thought, our feelings both reasonable and unreasonable, our imaginings, our beliefs, our happy and unhappy attachments, our secret desires with their contradictions, our experiences, suspicions, violence, and so on. The hidden ambitions, the illusions that the mind clings to, the superstitions of religion, and the seemingly everlasting conflict within ourselves are also part of our psychological structure. If we are blind to these, or accept them as an inevitable part of our human nature, we will allow a society in which we ourselves become prisoners. So this is really important to understand.

Surely every student throughout the world sees the effect of the chaos around us, and hopes to escape into some kind of outward order, even though in himself he may be in utter turmoil. He wants to change the outer without changing himself, but he is the source and continuation of the disorder. This is a fact, not a personal conclusion. So we are concerned in our education with changing the source of the disorder and its continuation. It is human beings who create society, not some gods in some heaven.

So we begin with the student. The very word implies studying, learning and acting. Basic education is to learn not only from books and teachers, but to study and learn about yourself. If you don't know about yourself, and are filling your mind with the facts of the universe, you are merely accepting and continuing the disorder. Probably as a student you are not interested in this. You want to enjoy yourself, pursue your own interests. You are forced to study, and do so only under pressure, accepting the inevitable comparisons and results with an eye fixed on some kind of career. This is your basic interest, which seems natural, because your parents and grandparents have followed the same path – job, marriage, children, responsibility. As long as you are safe, you care little for what is happening around you. This is your actual relationship to the world, the world human beings have created. The immediate is far more real, important and demanding for you than the whole.

But your concern and the educator's concern is and must be to understand the whole of human existence, not a part but the whole. The part is only the knowledge of human physical discoveries. So here, in these letters, we begin primarily with you, the student, and the educator who is helping you to know yourself. This is the function of all education. We need to bring about a good society in which all human beings can live happily in peace, without violence, with security. You as a student are responsible for this. A good society doesn't come into existence through some ideal, a hero or a leader, or some carefully planned system. You have to be good because you are the future. You will make the world, either as it is, modified, or as a world in which you and others can live without wars, without brutalities, with generosity and affection.

So what will you do? You have understood the problem, which is not difficult, so what will you do? Most of you are instinctively kind, good and wanting to help, unless of course you have been too trodden down and twisted, which one hopes you are not. So what will you do? If the educator is worth his salt, he will want to help you. Then the question is: what will you do together to help you to study yourself, to learn about yourself and act? We will stop here with this letter and go on in our next.

34. AFFECTION

*When you care, violence in every form
disappears from you*

To continue with what we were saying in our previous letter, we were pointing out your responsibility to study, to learn and to act. Since you are young and perhaps innocent, given to excitement and games, the word responsibility will seem rather frightening and a wearisome burden. But we are using the word to imply care and concern for our world. When we use this word, the students must not feel any sense of guilt if they have not shown this care and attention. After all, your parents who feel responsible for you, that you should study and equip yourselves for your future life, do not feel guilty, though they may feel disappointed or unhappy if you do not come up to their expectations. We must clearly understand that when we use the word responsibility there must not be a feeling of guilt. We are taking particular care to use this word free from the unhappy weight of a word like duty. When this is clearly understood, then we can use the word responsibility without its burden of tradition.

So, you are at school with this responsibility to study, to learn, to act. This is the main purpose of education.

In our previous letter we put the question: what will you do about yourself and your relationship with the world? As we said, the educator, the teacher, is responsible for helping you to understand yourself and so the world. We ask this question for you to find out for yourself what your response is. It is a challenge that you must answer. You have to begin with yourself, to understand yourself. In relation to that, what is the first step? Isn't it affection? Probably when you are young you have this quality, but very quickly you seem to lose it. Why? Is it because of the pressure of studies, the pressure of competition, the pressure of trying to reach a certain standing in your studies, comparing yourself with others, and perhaps being bullied by other students? Do not all these many pressures force you to be concerned with yourself? And when you are so concerned with yourself, you inevitably lose the quality of affection. It is very important to understand how circumstances – environment, the pressure of your parents or your own urge to conform – gradually narrow the vast beauty of life to the small circle of yourself. If you lose the quality of affection while you are young, there is a hardening of the heart and mind. It is a rare thing to keep this affection without corruption throughout life. So this is the first thing you must have.

Affection implies care, a diligent care in whatever you are doing – care in your speech, in your dress, in the manner of your eating, how you look after your body; care in your behaviour without distinctions of superior or inferior, how you consider people. Politeness is consideration for others, and this consideration is care, whether it is for your younger brother or oldest sister. When you care, violence in every form disappears from you – your anger, your antagonism and your pride. This care implies attention. Attention is to watch, observe, listen, learn. There are many things you can learn from books, but there is a learning which is infinitely clear, quick and without any ignorance. Attention implies sensitivity, and this gives depth to perception, which no knowledge, with its related ignorance, can give. This you have to study, not in a book, but with the help of the educator learn to observe things around you – what is happening in the world; what is happening with a fellow student; what is happening in a poor village or slum and to the man who is struggling along a dirty street.

Observation is not a habit. It isn't a thing you train yourself to do mechanically. It is the fresh eye of interest, of care, of sensitivity. You cannot train yourself to be sensitive. When you are young you are sensitive, quick in your perceptions, but this fades as you grow older. So you have to study yourself, and perhaps your teacher will help you. If he doesn't, it doesn't matter, because it is your responsibility to study yourself and so learn what you are. And when there is affection, your actions will be born out of its purity. All this may sound very hard, but it is not. We have neglected all this side of life.

We are so concerned with our careers, with our own pleasures, with our own importance, that we neglect the great beauty of affection.

There are two words that one must continually bear in mind – diligence and negligence. We diligently apply our mind to acquiring knowledge from books, from teachers; we spend twenty or more years of our life in that, and neglect to study the deeper meaning of our own life itself. We have both the outer and the inner. The inner demands greater diligence than the outer. It is an urgent demand. And this diligence is in the affectionate study of what one is.

35. SEEING THE FACT

People live with ideas and beliefs
unrelated to their daily lives

Cruelty is an infectious disease, and one must strictly guard one-self against it. Some students seem to have this peculiar infection, and they somehow gradually dominate the others. Probably they feel it is very manly, for their elders are often cruel in their words, in their attitudes, in their gestures, in their pride. This cruelty exists in the world. The responsibility of the student – and please remember with what significance we are using that word responsibility – is to avoid any form of cruelty.

Once, many years ago, I was invited to talk at a school in California, and as I entered the school a boy of ten or so was passing me with a large bird whose broken legs were caught in a trap. I stopped and looked at the boy without saying a word. His face expressed fear, and when I finished the talk and came out, the boy, a stranger, came up to me with tears in his eyes and said, 'Sir, it will never happen again'. He was afraid that I would tell the headmaster and there would be a scene about it; but because I didn't say a word either to the boy or to the headmaster about the cruel incident, his awareness of the terrible thing he had done made him realize the enormous-ness of the act.

It is important to be aware of our own activities. If there is affection, then cruelty has no place in our life at any time. In Western countries, you see birds carefully nurtured and later in the season shot for sport and then eaten. The cruelty of hunting, killing small animals, has become part of our civilization, like war, like torture, and the acts of terrorists and kidnappers. In our intimate personal relationships, there is also a great deal of cruelty, anger, hurting each other.

The world has become a dangerous place in which to live. In our schools any form of coercion, threat, anger must be totally and com-pletely avoided, for all these harden the heart and mind, and affection cannot coexist with cruelty. You understand, as a student, how important it is to realize that any form of cruelty not only hardens your heart but it also perverts your thinking, distorts your actions. The mind, like the heart, is a delicate instrument, sensitive and very capable, and when cruelty and oppression touch it, then there is a hardening of the self. Affection, love, has no centre as the self.

Now, having read this and having understood so far what is said, what will you do about it? You have studied what has been said; you are learning the content of these words. What then is your action? Your response is not merely to study and learn, but also to act. Most of us know and are aware of all the implications of cruelty and of what it actually does both outwardly and inwardly. We leave it at that without doing anything about it, thinking one thing and doing just the opposite. This not only breeds a great deal of conflict, but also hypocrisy. Most students do not like to be hypocrites: they like to look at facts, but they do not always act. So the responsibility of the student is to see the facts about cruelty, and without any persuasion or cajoling to understand what is implied and do something about it. The doing is perhaps a greater responsibility. People generally live with ideas and beliefs totally unrelated to how they conduct their daily life, and so this naturally becomes hypocrisy. So don't be a hypocrite, which doesn't mean you must be rude, aggressive or overly critical. When there is affection, there is inevitably courtesy without hypocrisy.

What is the responsibility of the teacher – who has studied, learnt and acts – toward the student? Cruelty has many forms: it can be in a look, a gesture, a sharp remark, and above all in comparison. Our whole educational system is based on comparison. We say that A is better than B, and so B must conform to or imitate A. This in essence is cruelty, ultimately expressed in examinations. What is the responsibility of the educator who sees the truth of this? How will he teach any subject without using reward and punishment, knowing that there must be some kind of report indicating the capacity of the student? Can the teacher do this? Is it compatible with affection? If the central reality of affection is there, has comparison any place at all? Can the teacher eliminate in himself the pain of comparison? Our whole civilization is based on hierarchical comparison both out-wardly and inwardly which denies the sense of deep affection. Can we eliminate from our minds the better, the more, the stupid, the clever, this whole comparative thinking? If the teacher has under-stood the pain of comparison, what is his responsibility in his teach-ing and in his action?

A person who has really grasped the significance of the pain of comparison is acting from intelligence.

36. REWARD AND PUNISHMENT

Action based on reward and punishment
brings about conflict

In all these letters we have been constantly pointing out that co-operation between the educator and the student is the responsibility of both. The word cooperation implies working together, but we cannot work together if we are not looking in the same direction with the same eyes and the same mind. The word same, as we are using it, under no circumstances implies uniformity, conformity or accepting, obeying, imitating. In cooperation with each other, working together, the student and the teacher must have a relationship which is essentially based on affection. Most people cooperate if they are building, if they are playing games, or are involved in scientific research, or if they are working together for an ideal, a belief, or for some concept which is carried out for some personal or collective benefit. Or they cooperate around a religious or political authority.

To study, learn, and act, cooperation is necessary between the teacher and the student. Both are involved. The educator may know many subjects and facts, but conveying them to the student becomes a struggle between the two if there is not the quality of affection. We are concerned not only with knowledge of the world but also with the study of oneself, in which learning and action are involved. Both the educator and the student are involved in this, and here authority ceases. To learn about himself, the educator is concerned not only with himself but with the student. In this interaction with its reactions, one begins to see the nature of oneself – the thoughts, the desires, the attachments, the identifications, and so on. Each is acting as a mirror to the other; each is observing in the mirror exactly what he is, because, as we pointed out earlier, the psychological understanding of oneself is far more important than gathering facts and storing them up as knowledge for skill in action. The inner always overcomes the outer. This must be clearly understood both by the educator and by the student. The outer has not changed man; the outer activities – physical revolution, physical control of the environment – have not deeply changed the human being, his prejudices and superstitions. Deeply, human beings remain as they have been for thousands of years. Right education is to transform this basic condition. When this is really grasped by the educator, though he may have subjects to teach, his main concern must be with the radical revolution in the psyche, in the "you" and the "me".

And here comes in the importance of cooperation between the two who are studying, learning and acting together. It is not the spirit of a team, or the spirit of a family, or identification with a group or nation. It is free inquiry into ourselves, without the barrier of the one who knows and the one who doesn't. This is the most destructive barrier, especially in matters of self-knowing. There is no leader and no led in this matter. When this is fully grasped, and with affection, then communication between the student and the teacher becomes easy, clear and is not at a merely verbal level. Affection carries no pressure; it is never devious. It is direct and simple.

Having said all this, and if both of you have studied what has been said, what is the quality of your mind and heart? Is there a change that is not induced by influence or by mere stimulation which may give an illusion of change? Stimulation is like a drug: it wears off and you are back where you were. Any form of pressure or influence also acts in the same way. If you act under these circumstances, you are not actually studying and learning about yourself. Action based on reward and punishment, influence or pressure, inevitably brings about conflict. This is so, but few people see the truth of this, and so they give up, or say it is impossible in a practical world, or that it is idealistic, some utopian concept. But it is not. It is eminently practical and workable. So do not be put off by the traditionalists, the conservatives, or those who cling to the illusion that change can come only from without.

When you study and learn about yourself, there comes an extraordinary strength, based on clarity, which can withstand all the nonsense of the Establishment. This strength is not a form of resistance or self-centred obstinacy or will, but is a diligent observation of the outer and the inner. It is the strength of affection and intelligence.

37. COMMUNICATION

Communication is learning
from each other

You come to these schools with your own background, traditional or free, with discipline or without discipline, obeying or reluctant and disobeying, in revolt or conforming. Your parents are either negligent or very diligent about you. Some may feel very responsible, others may not. You come with all this trouble, with broken families, uncertain or assertive, wanting your way or shyly acquiescing but inwardly rebelling.

In these schools you are free, and all the disturbances of your young lives come into play. You want your own way and no one in the world can have his or her own way. You have to understand this very seriously; you cannot have your own way. Either you learn to adjust with understanding, with reason, or you are broken by the new environment you have entered. It is very important to understand this.

In these schools the educators explain things carefully, and you can discuss with them, have a dialogue and see why certain things have to be done. When one lives in a small community of teachers and students, it is necessary that they have a good relationship with each other that is friendly, affectionate, and has a certain quality of attentive comprehension. No one, especially nowadays living in a free society, likes rules, but rules become totally unnecessary when you and the grown-up educator understand, not only verbally and intellectually but with your heart, that certain disciplines are necessary. The word discipline has been ruined by the authoritarians. Each craft has its own discipline, its own skill. The word discipline comes from the word disciple which means to learn – to learn, not to conform, not to rebel, but to learn about your own reactions and your own background and how those limit you, and to go beyond them.

The essence of learning is constant movement without a fixed point. If its point becomes your prejudice, your opinions and conclusions, and you start from this handicap, then you cease to learn. Learning is infinite. The mind that is constantly learning is beyond all knowledge. So you are here to learn as well as to communicate.

Communication is not only the exchange of words, however articulate and clear those words may be; it is much deeper than that. Communication is learning from each other, understanding each other; and this comes to an end when you have taken a definite stand about some trivial or not fully thought-out act.

When one is young, there is an urge to conform, not to feel out of things. To learn the nature and implications of conformity brings its own peculiar discipline. Please always bear in mind when we use that word discipline that both the student and the educator are in a relationship of learning, not assertion and acceptance. When this is clearly understood, rules become unnecessary. When this is not clear, then rules have to be made. You may revolt against rules, against being told what to do or not to do, but when you quickly understand the nature of learning, rules will disappear altogether. It is only the obstinate, the self-assertive, who bring about rules – thou shalt and thou shalt not.

Learning is not born out of curiosity. You may be curious about sex. That curiosity is based on pleasure, on some kind of excitement, on the attitudes of others. The same applies to drinking, drugs, smoking. Learning is far deeper and more extensive. You learn about the universe not out of pleasure or curiosity, but out of your relationship to the world. We have divided learning into separate categories depending on the demands of society or your own personal inclination. We are not talking of learning about something, but the quality of the mind that is willing to learn. You can learn how to become a good carpenter or a gardener or an engineer. When you have acquired skill in these, you have narrowed down your mind into a tool that can function perhaps skilfully in a certain pattern. This is what is called learning. This gives a certain security financially, and perhaps that is all one wants, so we create a society which provides what we have asked of it. But when there is this extra quality of learning that is not about something, then you have a mind and, of course, a heart that are timelessly alive.

Discipline is not control or subjugation. Learning implies attention; that is, to be diligent. It is only the negligent mind that is never learning. It is forcing itself to accept when it is shallow, careless, indifferent. A diligent mind is actively watching, observing, never sinking into second-hand values and beliefs. A mind that is learning is a free mind, and freedom demands the responsibility of learning. The mind that is caught in its own opinions, that is entrenched in some knowledge, may demand freedom, but what it means by freedom is the expression of its own personal attitudes and conclusions – and when this is thwarted it cries for self-fulfilment. Freedom has no sense of fulfilment. It is free.

So when you come to these schools, or to any school in fact, there must be this gentle quality of learning, and with it goes a great sense of affection. When you are really, deeply affectionate you are learning.

38. EDUCATING ONESELF

*To learn about the images we have
demands self-awareness*

Every profession has its discipline, every action has its direction, and every thought has its end. This is the cycle in which the human mind is caught. Being a slave to the known, the mind is always trying to expand its knowledge, its action within that field, its thought seeking its own end. In all schools, discipline is regarded as a framework for the mind and its action, and in recent years there has been revolt against any form of control, restraint or moderation. This has led to every form of permissiveness, immodesty and the pursuit of pleasure at any cost. Nobody has any respect for anyone. It appears that all forms of personal dignity and deep integrity have been lost. Billions are spent on drugs, on destroying bodies and minds. This all-permissiveness has become respectable and accepted as the norm of life.

To cultivate a good mind, a mind that is capable of perceiving the whole of life as one unit, unbroken and so a good mind, it is necessary that in all our schools a certain kind of discipline must exist. We must together understand the hated and perhaps despised words discipline and rules.

To learn you need to have attention. To learn there must be not only hearing with the ear, but an inward grasp of what is being said. To learn it is necessary to observe. When you hear or read these statements you have to give an attention that is not compelled, and not be under any pressure or expectation of reward or punishment. Discipline means to learn, not to conform. If you want to be a good carpenter, you must learn about the proper tools to use with different kinds of wood, and learn from a master carpenter. If you wish to be a good doctor, you must study for many years, learn all the facts of the body and its many ways, cures, and so on. Every profession demands that you learn as much about it as you possibly can.

This learning is to accumulate knowledge about it and act as skilfully as you can.

Learning is the nature of discipline. Learning why one should be punctual for meals, the proper time for rest and so on is learning about order in life. In a disorderly world where there is much confusion politically, socially and even in religion, our schools must be centres of order for the education of intelligence. A school is a sacred place where all are learning about the complexity of life and its simplicity.

So learning demands application and order. Discipline is never conformity, so don't be afraid of the word and rebel against it. Words have become very important in our life. The word God has become extraordinarily important to most people, or the word nation, or the name of a politician. The word is the image of the politician. The image of God has been built by thousands of years of thought and fear. We live with images created by the mind or by a skilful hand. To learn about these images that one has accepted or self-created demands self-awareness.

Education is not only learning about academic subjects but educating oneself.

39. EFFICIENCY

Efficiency is not an end in itself

A school is a place of learning, and so it is sacred. The temples, churches and mosques are not sacred for they have stopped learning. They believe; they have faith, and that denies entirely the great art of learning. A school, like those to which this letter is sent, must be devoted entirely to learning, not only about the world around us, but essentially about what we human beings are, why we behave the way we do, and the complexity of thought.

The ancient tradition of mankind has been learning, not only from books, but about the nature and structure of the psychology of a human being. As we have neglected this, there is disorder in the world, terror, violence and all the cruel things that are taking place. We have put the world's affairs first and not the inner. The inner, if it is not understood, educated and transformed, will always overcome the outer, however well organized the outer may be politically, economically and socially. This is a truth which many seem to forget. We are trying politically, legally and socially to bring order in the outer world in which we are living, and inwardly we are confused, uncertain, anxious and in conflict. Without inward order there will always be danger to human life.

What do we mean by order? In the supreme sense, the universe has known no disorder. Nature, however terrifying to man, is always in order. It becomes disordered only when human beings interfere with it. It is only man from the beginning of time who seems to be in constant struggle and conflict. The universe has its own movement of time. Only when man has ordered his life will he realize the eternal order.

Why has humanity accepted and tolerated disorder? Why does whatever man touches decay, become corrupt and confused? Why has mankind turned away from the order of nature, the clouds, the winds, the animals and the rivers? We must learn what disorder is and what order is. Disorder is essentially conflict, self-contradiction and division between becoming and being. Order is a state in which disorder has never existed.

Disorder is bondage to time. Time to us is very important. We live in the past, in past memories, past hurts and pleasures. Our thought is the past. It is always modifying itself as a reaction to the present, projecting itself into the future, but the deep-rooted past is always with us. This is the binding quality of time. We must observe this fact in ourselves and be aware of its limiting process. That which is limited must ever be in conflict.

The past is knowledge derived from experience, action and psychological responses. This knowledge, of which one may be conscious or not aware, is the very nature of man's existence. So the past becomes all-important, whether it is tradition, experience, or remembrance with its many images. But all knowledge, whether in the future or the past, is limited. There can be no complete knowledge. Knowledge and ignorance go together.

In learning about this, that very learning is order. Order is not something planned and adhered to. In a school, routine is necessary, but this is not order. A machine that is well put together functions efficiently. The efficient organization of a school is absolutely necessary, but this efficiency is not an end in itself to be confused with the freedom from conflict which is order.

How will an educator, if he has deeply learnt all this, convey the nature of order to the student? If his own inward life is in disorder and he talks about order, he will not only be a hypocrite, which in itself is a conflict, but the student will realize that what is being said is double talk and so will not pay the least attention to it. When the educator is immovable in his understanding, the student will grasp that very quality. When one is completely honest, that very honesty is transmitted to another.

40. THINKING TOGETHER

*Freedom is the essence
of thinking together*

I think it is important to learn the art of thinking together. Scientists and the most uneducated human beings think. They think according to their profession, specialization and according to their beliefs and experiences. We all think, objectively or according to our own particular inclinations, but we never seem to think together, to observe together. We may think about something, a particular problem or an experience, but this thinking does not go beyond its own limitation. Thinking together, not about a particular subject but having the capacity to think together, is entirely different. To think together is necessary when you are facing the great crisis that is taking place in the world, the danger, the terror and the ultimate brutality of war. To observe this, not as a capitalist, socialist, from the extreme left or extreme right, but to observe it together, demands not only that we comprehend how we have come to this rotten state, but also that together we perceive a way out. The businessman or the politician looks at this problem from a limited point of view, but we are saying we must look at life as a whole not as British, French or Chinese.

What does it mean to look at life as a whole? It means to observe the human being, ourselves, without any division of nationality, to see life as one single movement without a beginning and without an end, without time, without death. This is a difficult thing to understand because we think of the part, not the totality. We divide, hoping to understand the whole from its part.

The art of thinking together needs to be studied carefully, examined to see whether it is at all possible. Each one clings to his own way of thinking according to his own particular reactions, experiences, prejudices. This is how we are conditioned, and it prevents having the capacity to think together. Thinking together does not mean being of one mind. Our minds can come together about an ideal, an historical conclusion or some philosophical concept, and work for that, but this is essentially based on authority. Freedom is the essence of thinking together. You must be free from your concepts, prejudices, and so on. I too must be free, and we come together in this freedom. It means dropping all our conditioning. It implies complete attention without any past. The present world crisis demands that we totally abandon our tribal instincts that have become glorified as nationalism. Thinking together implies that we totally abandon self-interest and identifying ourselves as British, Arab, Russian, and so on.

Then what is a human being to do facing this danger of the separatism of self-interest? There is the expansionist movement of one power over another economically or politically, or of one or two bigoted, neurotic leaders. What is a human being confronted with this to do? Either you turn away from it and withdraw into indifference, or you join some political activity, or take refuge in some religious group. You cannot escape from this. It is there.

What do I do? I reject the present pattern of social structures, the nonsensical irreligious ways. I reject all that. So I am totally isolated. This isolation is not an escape to some form of ivory tower or into some romantic illusion. Because I see the futility, the divisiveness in the pursuit of self-interest and nationalism, in expansionism, in the irreligious life, I reject the total destructiveness of this society. So I stand alone. As I am not then contributing psychologically to the destructive consciousness of man, I am in the stream of that which is goodness, compassion and intelligence. That intelligence is acting, confronting the madness of the present world. That intelligence will act wherever the ugly is.

41. ATTENTION

*Awareness brings about
subtlety, clarity of mind*

We ought to consider together what we mean by attention. Most of us learn what concentration is; from childhood we are compelled to concentrate on something, which generally we don't like. This breeds a kind of rebellion from being forced to do something we dislike. Education has become a funnelling of many subjects into our brains, conditioning us to conform. Millions throughout the world are being educated but are finding no jobs. The whole pattern of society in which we live has become so abnormal, so dangerous, that we must find a new way of living together. This requires sensitivity and very objective observation and thinking. One questions whether concentration, which is the narrowing down of perception, will help to bring about a different quality of mind.

For what are you being educated? What are you going to become as a human being? Mediocrity prevails from the highest political structure to the highest religious establishment. Are you being educated to fit into this pattern? Are you going to become a mediocre human being without any passion, in conflict with yourself and with the world? This is really a serious question you have to ask yourself. Can concentrated, aggressive, competitive human beings bring about a different order in our existence?

As we said, we ought to consider what it means to be attentive. This may be the clue to a harmonious existence. As things are, the intellect, the whole activity of the brain, which is thinking, dominates our existence. This brings about contradiction, peculiar behaviour in us. When only one part of our whole being is dominant, it will inevitably bring about neurotic behaviour. Attention is awareness of this dominance of intellect without acting on the instinctive urge to control it or to allow emotion to take its place. This awareness brings about subtlety, clarity of mind.

There is a difference between concentration and attention. Concentration is to bring all your energy to focus on a particular point. In attention there is no point of focus. We are very familiar with one and not with the other. When you pay attention to your body, the body becomes quiet, has its own discipline; it is relaxed but not slack and it has the energy of harmony. When there is attention there is no contradiction and therefore no conflict.

As you read this, pay attention to the way you are sitting, to the way you are listening, to how you are receiving what the letter is saying to you, to how you are reacting to what is being said and to why you are finding it difficult to attend. You are not learning how to attend. If you are learning the "how" of attending, then it becomes a system, which is what the brain is accustomed to, and so you make attention something mechanical and repetitive. But attention is not mechanical or repetitive. It is the way of looking at your whole life without the centre of self-interest.

42. FAMILY AND SOCIETY

*Is life a movement of pain
with occasional happiness?*

The future for every human being, the young and the old, appears to be bleak and frightening. Society itself has become dangerous and utterly immoral. When a young person faces the world, he is rather frightened of what will happen to him in the course of his life. His parents send him to school and, if they have money, to university, and they are concerned that he should settle down to a job, marry, have children, and so on. In families in the Eastern world the parents play a strong part in their children's lives. The family unit is still there, and though the young may earn livelihoods in different parts of the world, the family is the centre of their lives. This is fast disappearing in the Western world. In many parts of the world parents have very little time for their own children. A few years after the children are born the parents have lost them; they have very little relationship with their children. They worry about their own problems, ambitions, and so on, and the children are at the mercy of educators, who themselves need education. The educators may be excellent at academics and are in turn concerned that their students should achieve the highest academic grades and that the school should have the best reputation. But educators have their own problems. Their salaries, except in a few countries, are rather low, and socially they are not highly regarded.

Those who are being educated have rather a difficult time with their parents, their educators and their fellow students. Already the tide of struggle, of anxiety, fear and competition has swept in. They have to face a world that is overpopulated, with undernourished people, a world of war, increasing terrorism, inefficient governments, corruption and the threat of poverty. This threat is less evident in affluent and fairly well-organized societies, but it is felt in those parts of the world where there is tremendous poverty, overpopulation and the indifference of inefficient rulers. This is the world the young people have to face, and naturally they are really frightened. They have an idea that they should be free, independent of routine, should not be dominated by their elders; and they shy away from all authority. Freedom to them means to choose what they want to do; but they are confused, uncertain and want to be shown what they should do. The student is caught between his own desire for freedom to do what he wants and society's demands for conformity to its own necessities – that people become engineers, scientists, soldiers, or specialists of some kind. This is the world students have to face and become a part of through their education. It is a frightening world. We all want security physically as well as emotionally, and having this is becoming more and more difficult and painful.

So we of the older generation, if we at all care for our children, must ask what education is. If education, as it is now universally, is to prepare the children to live in perpetual striving, conflict and fear, we must ask what the meaning of it all is. Is life a movement, a flow of pain and anxiety and the shedding of unshed tears, with occasional flares of joy and happiness? Unfortunately we, the older generation, do not ask these questions, and neither does the educator. So education, as it is now, is a process of facing a dreary, narrow and meaningless existence. But we want to give a meaning to life. Life appears to have no meaning in itself, but we want to give it meaning, so we invent gods, various forms of religion and other entertainments, including nationalism and ways to kill each other, in order to escape from our monotonous life. This is the life of the older generation and will be the life of the young.

We the parents and educators have to face this fact and not escape into theories, seeking further forms of education and structures. If our minds are not clear about what we are facing, we shall inevitably, consciously or unconsciously, slip into the inaction of wondering what to do about it. There are a thousand people who will tell us what to do: the specialists and the cranks. Before we understand the vast complexity of the problem, we want to operate upon it. We are more concerned to act than to see the whole issue.

The real issue is the quality of our mind – not its knowledge, but the depth of the mind that meets knowledge. Mind is infinite, is the nature of the universe, which has its own order, has its own immense energy. It is everlastingly free. The brain, as it is now, is the slave of knowledge and so is limited, finite, fragmentary. When the brain frees itself from its conditioning, then the brain is infinite. Then only is there no division between the mind and the brain. Education then is freedom from conditioning, from the vast accumulated knowledge of tradition. This does not deny the value of academic disciplines, which have their own proper place in life.

43. THE VASTNESS OF LIFE

The movement of the skies, the earth,
human existence, is indivisible

We have said that education must not only be efficient in academic disciplines but that it must also explore the conditioning of human conduct. This conduct is the result of many, many centuries of fear, anxiety, conflict and the search for security both inwardly and outwardly, both biologically and psychologically. The brain is conditioned by these processes. The brain is the result of evolution, which is time. We are the result of the accumulated past both religiously and in our daily life. It is based on reward and punishment as an animal, a dog is trained.

Our brain is an extraordinary instrument of great energy and capacities. Look at what it has done in the outward world, in the world that surrounds us. It has divided it into various races, religions and nationalities. It has done this to have security. It has sought this security in religious, political and economic isolation, and in the unit of the family, in small communities and associations. It has sought this protective reaction in organizations and establishments.

Nationalism has been one of the major causes of war. Our politicians are concerned with maintaining economic nationalism, and thus they isolate us. Where there is isolation there must be opposition, aggression, and any good relationship with other nations appears to be based on trade, exchange of armaments, the balance of power, and maintaining power in the hands of the few. This is our government, whether totalitarian or democratic. We have sought to bring about order in society through political action, and so we have become dependent upon the politicians. Why have politicians become so extraordinarily important, like gurus, like the religious leaders? Is it because we have always depended on outside agencies to put our house in order, always depended on external forces to control and shape our lives? The external authority of a govern-

135

ment, of parents, of every form of specialized leader seems to give us some hope for the future. This is part of our tradition of dependence and acceptance. This has been the long accumulated tradition that has conditioned our brain. Education has accepted this, and so the brain has become mechanical and repetitive.

Isn't it the function of the educator to understand the tremendous accumulated energy of the past, without denying its necessity in certain areas of our lives? Aren't we concerned as educators to bring about the flowering of good human beings? This is not possible when the past, however modified, continues.

What then are the factors of our conditioning? What is it that is being conditioned, and who is it who does the conditioning? When we ask these questions, are we aware of our own actual conditioning, and from that awareness asking the questions, which would have great vitality; or are we asking a theoretical question? We are not concerned in any way with hypothetical questions; we are dealing with actualities, the actual being what is. We are asking what the cause is of this state of human beings. There may be one cause or many causes. Many little streams give their waters to a great river. The depth, the volume and the beauty are all-important, not tracing each little stream to its source. So we are concerned in our investigation with the totality of our existence, not a particular part of it. When we comprehend the vastness of life with its complexities, then only can we ask what the cause of our conditioning is.

One feels it is important to understand first, not verbally or intellectually, but to perceive that life is the woman, the man, the child, the animals, the river, the sky and the forest – all of it – to feel this, not the idea of it, but to see the immensity and beauty of it. If we do not grasp the significance of this – that all the vast movement of life is one – when we ask what the cause of conditioning is, we bring about the fragmentation of life. So, first, let us realize that the movement of the skies, the earth, human existence, is indivisible, and only then come to the particular. When the heavens, the earth and human beings are seen as one vast unitary process, then inquiry as to the cause of our conditioning will not be fragmentary, divisive.

Then we can ask what the cause is. Then the question has depth and beauty.

To find the cause of conditioning, we must inquire together into its nature and structure. Apart from the biological, the organic, which left to itself has its own natural intelligence, its self-protective reactions, there is the whole psychological field of a human being, the inward responses, inward hurts, the fears, the contradictions, the drive of desire, the passing pleasures and the weight of sorrow. This psyche, when it is disorderly, confused and messy, naturally affects the biological existence. Then disease is psychosomatic. Aren't we concerned with the exploration of our inward nature, which is very complex? This investigation is really self-education, not to change what is, but to understand what is. It is important to grasp, to live with this. What is is far more important than what should be. The understanding of what we actually are is far more essential than to transcend what we are. We are the content of our consciousness. Our consciousness is a complexity, but its very substance is movement. It must be clearly understood that we are not dealing with theories, hypotheses, ideals, but with our own actual daily existence.

44. AWARENESS

To attend implies vast energy

As we have pointed out, we are deeply involved in our daily life as educators and as human beings. We are human beings first and then educators, not the other way round. Because a teacher is a human being whose special profession is education, his life is not only in the classroom but is involved with the whole outer world as well as inner struggles, ambitions and relationships. He is as conditioned as the student. Though their conditioning may vary, it is still conditioning. If you accept it as inevitable and abide by it, then you are further conditioning others. There are many who accept this, trying to modify their limitations. But as educators aren't you concerned with bringing about a different social entity, a future generation which perceives the futility of wars as organized murder, a generation which is concerned with global interrelationship without nationalistic isolation, a generation which is involved with truth? Surely this is the function of a true educator.

Human consciousness is conditioned. Any thoughtful person would accept this fact, but many of us are not aware of this, and perhaps neither is the educator. To become aware of his conditioning, and to investigate whether it is possible to be free of its limitation, is one of the functions of a teacher. So we have to go into what it is to be aware, to concentrate, to give total attention. It is very important to understand the meaning of these.

Awareness implies sensitivity: to be sensitive to nature, to the hills, rivers and the trees around one; to be aware of a poor man walking down the road and to be sensitive to his feelings, his reactions, to his appalling and degrading poverty; to be sensitive to the man who is sitting next to you, or to the nervousness of your friend or sister. This sensitivity has no choice in it and it does not criticize. There is no judgemental evaluation.

You are sensitive to a cloud about which you can do nothing. Is this sensitivity the result of time and practice? If you allow thought and practice, then that very thought and practice kill sensitivity. Learn to observe sensitively; learn what sensitivity implies; capture it rather than cultivate it. Don't ask how to capture it – grasp it. In the very perception you are sensitive. There is no resistance in sensitivity. Sensitivity is to the immediate and limitless.

Concentration is a process of resistance. Every educator knows what it means to concentrate. The educator is concerned with stuffing the brain with knowledge of various subjects so that the student will pass examinations and get a job. The student also has this in his mind. The educator and the student are encouraging each other in the form of resistance which is concentration. So one is building the capacity to resist, to exclude; and gradually one becomes isolated. Concentration is the focusing of one's energy on the blackboard or a book and avoiding distraction. The very word distraction implies concentration. Actually, there is no distraction; there is only resistance which is called concentration, and any movement away from that is considered distraction. So in this there is conflict, struggle and resistance. This resistance will inevitably bring about the limitation of the brain that is our conditioning. To perceive this whole movement with sensitivity is to move into a different area, which is to be attentive.

What is it to be attentive? If we really grasp the significance of sensitivity, of awareness, the limitation of concentration – not intellectually or verbally, but the actuality of such states – then we can ask what it is to be attentive. Attention involves seeing and hearing. We not only hear with our ears but we are also sensitive to the tones, to the voice, to the implication of words, to hear without interference, to capture instantly the depth of a sound. Sound plays an extraordinary part in our lives: the sound of thunder, a flute playing in the distance, the unheard sound of the universe, the sound of silence, the sound of one's own heart beating, the sound of a bird or a waterfall and the noise of a man walking on the pavement. The universe is filled with sound. This sound has its own silence; all living things are involved in this sound of silence. To be attentive is to hear this silence and move with it.

Seeing is a very complex affair. One sees casually with one's eyes, and swiftly passes by, never seeing the details of a leaf, its form and structure, its colours, the variety of greens. To observe a cloud with all the light of the world in it; to follow a stream chattering down the hill; to look at your friend with the sensitivity in which there is no resistance; and to see yourself as you are without the shades of denial or easy acceptance; to see yourself as part of the whole; to see the immensity of the universe – this is observation: to see without the shadow of yourself.

Attention is this hearing and this seeing, and this attention has no resistance, so it is limitless. To attend implies vast energy; it is not pinned down to a point. In this attention there is no repetitive movement; it is not mechanical. There is no question of how to maintain this attention. When one has learnt the art of seeing and hearing, this attention can focus itself on a page, a word. In this there is no resistance, which is the activity of concentration.

Inattention cannot be refined into attention. To be aware of inattention is the ending of it; it is not that it becomes attentive. The ending has no continuity. The past modifying itself is the future, a continuity of what has been. We find security in continuity, not in endings. So attention has no quality of continuity. Anything that continues is mechanical. Becoming is mechanical and implies time. Attention has no quality of time. All this is a tremendously complicated issue. One must gently, deeply go into it.

45. THE TEACHER

A teacher is deeply involved
with the flowering of human beings

We seem to think that education stops when we leave school or college. We seem not to treat the whole of human existence as a process of self-education that is constant and perhaps never-ending. Most of us limit education to a very short period, and for the rest of our lives carry on in rather a muddle, learning only a few things that are absolutely necessary, falling into a routine – and of course there is always death waiting. This is our life really: marriage, children, work, passing pleasures, pain and death. If this is our whole life, which apparently it is, then what really is the meaning of education?

We never ask these fundamental questions; probably they are too disturbing. But as we are teachers in colleges and schools, we must ask what the purpose of education and learning is. We know it is to prepare us for some sort of job and responsibilities, but apart from that preparation, what do we mean by teaching and what is the teacher? As it is generally understood, a teacher, having studied certain subjects, informs the student about them. Does this constitute being a teacher, just passing on knowledge? We are inquiring into the nature of the teacher and the taught. Who is a teacher? What are the implications of teaching apart from following the curricula? Very few people are dedicated teachers. They are dedicated to helping the students in their studies, but surely a teacher has far greater significance than that.

Knowledge must inevitably be superficial. It is the cultivation of memory and employing that memory efficiently, and so on. Since knowledge is always limited, is it the function of the teacher to help the student to live all his life only within the limitations of knowledge? We must first realize that knowledge is always limited, as are all experiences. This employment of knowledge with its limitations can be very destructive. It is destructive in human relationships. In relationships, knowledge, which is the accumulation of various in-

141

cidents, experiences, reactions, cultivates the image of the other person and obscures the reality of that person and of the relationship. When there is continuity, a tradition put together by knowledge and handed down from generation to generation, then the past, which is the accumulation of knowledge, obscures the actual living present. When knowledge becomes routine, mechanical, it makes the brain limited, rigid and insensitive. When knowledge is used for the support of nationalism through wars, then it becomes bestial, appallingly cruel and utterly immoral. Knowledge is not beauty, but knowledge is necessary to bore a well. The whole technological world is based on knowledge, and that world is taking over our lives. If we allow knowledge to be the sole authority, and hope through knowledge to ascend, then we are living in a fatal illusion. We are saying that knowledge has its place in everyday life, but when knowledge is the only substance of our life, then our life must be confined to mechanical activity.

Is the communication of knowledge the only function of the teacher: passing on information, ideas, theories and expanding on these theories in discussing various aspects of them? Is this the only function of a teacher? If this is all a teacher is concerned with, then he is merely a living computer. But surely a teacher has far greater responsibility than this. He must be concerned with behaviour, with the complexity of human action, with a way of life that is the flowering of goodness. Surely he must be concerned with the future of his students and what the future is for these students. What is the future of man? What is the future of our consciousness which is so confused, disturbed, messy, in conflict? Must we perpetually live in conflict, sorrow and pain? When the teacher is not in communication with the student about all these matters, then he is merely a living, clever machine perpetuating other machines.

So we are asking a very fundamental question: what is a teacher? Teaching is the greatest profession in the world, though the least respected, for if the teacher is deeply and seriously concerned, he is bringing about the unconditioning of the human brain, not only his own brain but the brains of the students. He is conditioned and the student is conditioned. Whether he admits it or not, this is a fact, and in relationship with the student he is helping both the student and himself to free consciousness from limitation.

A relationship is a process of learning. A relationship is not a static affair but a living movement. So it is never the same; what it was yesterday it is not today. When yesterday dominates in relationship, then relationship is what it was, not a living thing. Love is not what it was. When the relationship between the teacher and the student has this element of companionship, of mutual unconditioning and humility, sensitivity and affection are natural.

A teacher might say all this is impossible when school authorities demand that there be fifty students in a class and every kind of idiocy. Then what is a teacher to do? Obviously, in that situation he cannot do anything, but we are talking about schools where this does not take place, where the teacher can establish this relationship. And there he is deeply involved with the flowering of human beings.

46. VULNERABILITY

Without the centre as a self, there is
extraordinary strength and beauty

It appears that very few teachers are aware of their great responsibility not only to the parents, but also in their relationship to the students. What is this relationship? How does one regard this relationship? Is it communication of information? Is it the verbal statement of certain facts? Is the relationship superficial, casual and passing? Is the teacher an example? Am I as a teacher an influence? If I am an example that some of my students should follow, then I become a tyrant; then discipline becomes conformity. They imitate me, my ways, my gestures and so on. But I do not want them to follow me or be influenced by me. I want them to understand how all of us are influenced, moulded to conform to a pattern. My perception, my intention is to help my students to be free of every kind of influence, good or bad, so that they see for themselves what right action is; not be told what right action is, but to have the capacity and drive to see the false and the true. That is, my concern is primarily to cultivate their intelligence so that they can meet life with all its complexities intelligently. I see this not as a goal but as an immediate reality. I know they are influenced by their parents, by their fellow students and by the world around them. Young people are easily influenced. They may rebel against it but consciously or unconsciously there is pressure and the strain of this pressure. So I ask myself as a teacher, and as a human being, in what manner I can bring about the character and energy of intelligence.

I begin to see that I must be both introvert and extrovert in the world of action, and inwardly; not be self-centred but turn my eyes and my hearing to the subtleties of life. That is, I must be able to protect and at the same time cultivate generosity, be both the receiver and the giver. I feel all this if I am a really dedicated teacher in the true sense of that word. To me it is not a profession; it is something that has to be done. So I become very much more aware of the world, what is happening there, and inwardly comprehend the necessity to go beyond and above self-centred interest. I see this as a whole movement, the outward and the inward, indivisible like the waters of the sea that come in and go out. Now, how am I to help the student to be aware of this?

Sensitivity implies being vulnerable. One is sensitive to one's reactions, to one's hurts, one's beleaguered existence. That is, one is sensitive about oneself, and in this vulnerable state there is really self-interest and therefore the capability of being hurt, of becoming neurotic. It is a form of resistance, which is essentially concentrated in the self. The strength of vulnerability is not self-centred. It is like the young spring leaf that can withstand strong winds and flourish. This vulnerability is incapable of being hurt whatever the circumstances. Vulnerability is without a centre as the self. It has an extraordinary strength, vitality and beauty.

As a human being, in myself and as a teacher I see all this as clearly as possible. But as a teacher I am not all this. I am studying this, learning. As a teacher I am in relationship with my students, and in that relationship I am learning. In what manner am I to convey all this to my students who are conditioned, thoughtless, full of play, mischievous, as normal children are? I teach subjects and am wondering if I can convey all this through mathematics, biology, physics. Or are they separate, something to be memorized? I see that the intelligence is not from the cultivation of memory. So I have this problem: on the one hand I see the need for the cultivation of memory to pass examinations and ultimately for an occupation, and on the other hand I have a glimmer that intelligence is not mechanical, is not the cultivation of memory. This is my problem. I am asking myself if these two are separate, or if intelligence, if it is awakened from the very beginning of one's life, can include memory and not be a slave to it. The greater includes the lesser. The universe contains the particular. But the particular can only remain in its own narrow sphere.

I am beginning to comprehend this important factor, for I am a dedicated teacher who is using teaching as a stepping stone to something else. So I am wondering what to do with these children in front of me. They are not interested in all this. They bully each other, compete with each other; they are envious, and so on. Now, if you are not in the school, do you understand my problem? You have to, because you are also a teacher in your own way – at home, on the playing fields, or in business. We are all teachers in some way or other, so don't just leave me with my problem. It is your problem too, so let us talk about it.

We both see, I hope, that we are in this predicament: that it is of primary and greatest importance to bring about this intelligence in all children and in the students for whom we are responsible. Don't leave me alone to solve this problem; let us talk about it. First of all, I want you and me to understand the problem. Do we see that the student must eventually have an occupation, and so he must understand the world, the necessities of the world, its implicit disorder and its increasing destruction and decline? He has to face this world, but not as a specialized entity that makes him incapable of meeting the world. All this implies the acquisition of knowledge and the careful discipline of knowledge. As long as the world is what it is, he has to act in a certain direction and he is occupied most of the time with that, perhaps eight or ten hours a day. Also he has to study and learn about the whole psychological world which has not been explored fully by anyone. Those who have explored it somewhat say what they have discovered; but this becomes knowledge, and the student merely follows, which is not an accurate exploration into oneself.

So you and I have this issue. You may be casually interested, but I as a teacher am really concerned. I, too, am conditioned; I am not quite vulnerable in the sense that has been given here. I have my family problems and so on, but my dedication supersedes them all. What am I to do or not to do? Does it demand no action but to create with other teachers the atmosphere of intent? The intent is not a goal to be achieved sometime later. The intent is the ever-present activity in which time is not involved at all.

47. INTENTION

Our vital intent is to bring about
a free human being

Our intent is far more important than to achieve a goal, an end; it is not just toward an intellectual and ideological conclusion, but is an active, living present. It is the wick that is burning in a bowl of oil. It cannot be extinguished; no breeze can blow it out; the wick is stout, and the oil is not fed by any external influence or source. It has no cause, and so the flame, the wick and the oil are ever enduring. Our vital flame of intent is to bring about a good, intelligent, extremely capable, free human being. This is my intent as a dedicated teacher, and it should be yours, too, as parents. It should be the intent of all humanity, for we are all concerned. You cannot escape from this intention. You are involved in it as much as I am. You may shy away from it, disregard it, neglect it, but you are as much responsible as I am.

The future is our responsibility, so this is our immediate problem. My problem and yours is to cultivate the comprehensive intelligence from which all other things flow. I can see this in my mind's eye as the central factor, for no intelligent person, in the sense we are using that word, would ever want to hurt another intentionally. Such a person would treat all humanity as he would treat himself, without these terrible destructive divisions. I can also feel in some vague way, not sentimentally, that this intelligence is totally impersonal, neither yours nor mine. I can feel its tremendous attraction and its truth.

Now, in what manner can I cultivate this in my students and myself? I am using the wrong word cultivate – cultivation implies the activity of thought; it implies an achievement, a labour. So I am beginning to perceive that intelligence is totally different from the activity of thought. Thought has no relation to it. It cannot be born out of thought, for thought is always limited.

Now, having stated this, which is not a vague apprehension, but a burning intention, I ask myself if it is possible for me to convey to the student the quality of this intention, knowing that the students' brains are conditioned, limited, conforming. Can I do this through mathematics or biology, or any other subject?

Let us say I am a teacher of mathematics. Mathematics is order, infinite order. Order is the universe, is intelligence. Order is not static, it is a living movement. Our life is movement, but we have brought about disorder in our life. So I am going to talk to the students not just about mathematics, but about order in our life. Negation of disorder is order. A human being, being confused, disorderly, uncertain, in trying to establish order creates only more disorder. I see this very, very clearly, so I am going to help the students, and in helping them I am helping myself. That order cannot be pursued, as you can pursue mathematics, step by step. So the first thing to realize is that thought, do what it will, can never bring about order through legislation, administration or compulsion. Order is independent of thought. Thought cannot put together order; the more it attempts it, the greater the confusion. Mathematics is not disorder. Mathematics in itself is basically order. Thought is capable of seeing the order of mathematics, but this order is not the product of thought. One can see the great majesty and beauty of a mountain, but the human being who sees it may have no dignity, no majesty, no beauty.

I must study order and disorder before I can discuss it with my pupils. The study of a book on any particular subject is very different from the study of myself, who is disorderly, confused. The book reveals things phrase by phrase, chapter by chapter, coming to some conclusion or other. The book is visible, and one can spend perhaps years on the subject of the book. But I am not studying just any book; I am studying a book that has no print in it, one which cannot be read through another's eyes. So I must find out how to study it.

You are doing this with me too, so don't step aside. I am studying for my own interest and also to convey it to the student; it is not that I am studying for myself only. The book and the subject are palpable, tangible; the words convey a certain definite meaning. But to study the tenuous, living, changing subject that is the quality of my own brain, which lives in disorder, confusion and fear, is far more difficult than reading a book. It requires swiftness, subtlety, moving without leaving an imprint. Do I have such subtlety? In asking that question of myself, I am studying not only who puts that question but also the intent behind the question.

So I am studying the whole phenomenon very cautiously, never coming to a definite conclusion. This constant watchfulness, never allowing any shadow to slip by without careful observation, is making the brain, the whole activity of thought, quieten down without becoming dull. I take a rest and pick it up again. The rest is as important as the renewal of observation. I am capturing the perfume of that intelligence, the extraordinary subtlety of it, and so the whole physical organism is becoming more alive, aware, and is beginning to have a different rhythm. It is creating its own atmosphere.

Now I can go to the class under a tree or in a room where I am supposed to teach mathematics, knowing that the students have to qualify in it. For the first five or ten minutes, I talk to them, explaining very clearly what I have been studying and how it is possible for them to study it too. I am teaching them the art of studying. I am really deeply interested in conveying to them my deep intention, and they are enveloped in my ardour. I explain to them how I approach this question of intelligence step by step. I point out to them the order and beauty of a tree, which is not put together by thought. I insist that they see clearly that nature and the heavens and the wild animals of the forest are not the product of thought, although thought may use them for its own convenience or destruction. Thought in its activity has brought about great destruction and also great passing beauty. At every opportunity, without boring myself and the students, I talk about these matters with humour and seriousness. This is my life, for this intelligence is supreme.

Order has no cause, therefore it is everlasting; but disorder has a cause, and that which has a cause can end.

48. COMMITMENT

How are the few to deal with the many?

Discontent does not necessarily lead to intelligence. Most of us have some kind of dissatisfaction and are not satisfied with most things. We may have money, position and some kind of prestige in the world, but there is always this worm of discontent. The more you have, the more you want. Satisfaction is never satisfied. Discontent is like a flame; however much you feed it, it absorbs more. It is curious how easily satisfaction finds its temporary fulfilment, and one holds on to it, though it soon fades and the wanting more comes back again. It appears that this is the constant swing from one object of satisfaction to another, physically as well as inwardly. "The more" is the root of discontent. The flame of measurement leads either to satiety, indifference and neglect, or to a wider and deeper inquiry.

In inquiry, satisfaction is not the goal. Inquiry is its own source, which is never extinguished, and it can never forget itself through any kind of satisfaction. This flame can never be smothered by any outward or inward activity of achievement. Most of us have a tiny flame, which is generally smothered by some form of gain, but in order to allow this tiny flame to burn furiously, the measurement of "the more" must totally end. Then only does the flame burn away all sense of gratification.

As an educator, I have been concerned with another problem. I cannot have a school all to myself. In a school I have many colleagues. Some are extremely bright – I am not being patronizing – others are of varying dullness, though all are what is called well-educated, have degrees, and so on. Perhaps one or two of us are trying to help the students to understand the nature of intelligence, but I feel that unless all of us are together cooperatively helping the student in this direction, those teachers who are not concerned with the cultivation of it will act as an impediment. This is the problem of a few of us; this goes on most of the time in educational centres.

So my problem is – and again let me repeat that this is not being said in any patronizing way – how are we, the few, to deal with the many? What is our response to them? It is a challenge that must be met at all levels of our life. In all forms of government, there is the division between the few and the many. The few may be concerned with the whole population, and the many are concerned with their own particular little interests. This happens all over the world and it is happening in the field of education. So how are we to establish a relationship with those of us who are not totally committed to the flowering of intelligence and goodness? Or is it all one problem – to awaken the flame in the whole of the school?

Of course, the authoritarian attitude destroys all intelligence. The sense of obedience breeds only fear which in itself inevitably drives away the understanding of the true nature of intelligence. So what place has authority in a school? We have to study authority, not merely assert that there should be no authority but only freedom. We have to study it as we study the atom. The structure of the atom is orderly. Obedience, following, accepting authority, whether it is blind or clear-eyed, must inevitably bring about disorder. What is the root of obedience, which breeds authority? When one is in disorder, confusion, society becomes utterly chaotic; then that very disorder creates authority, as has happened so often historically. Is fear the root of accepting authority, being uncertain, without clarity in oneself? Then each human being helps to bring about the authority that will tell us what to do, as has happened in all religions, all sects and communities. It is the everlasting problem of the guru and the disciple, each destroying the other. The follower then becomes the leader. This cycle is forever repeating itself.

We are studying together, in the real sense of the word, what the cause of authority is. If each one of us sees that it is fear, muddle-headedness, or some deeper factor, then the mutual study of it, verbal or non-verbal, has significance. In studying, there may be an exchange of thought and the silent observation of the cause of authority. Then that very study uncovers the light of intelligence, for intelligence has no authority. It is not your intelligence or my intelligence. A few of us may see this deeply, without any deception,

151

and it is our responsibility that this flame be spread wherever we are, in school, at home, or in a bureaucratic government. It has no abiding place; it is wherever you are.

49. VISION

The ideal breeds conflict

Our brains are very old. They have evolved through countless experiences, accidents, death. The continuity of the flowering of the brain has been going on for millennia. It has varieties of capacities, is ever active, moving and living in its own memories and anxieties, full of fear, uncertainty and sorrow. This is the everlasting cycle it has lived, with passing pleasures and incessant activity. In this long process it has been conditioning itself, shaping its own way of life, adjusting itself to its own environment as few species have, combining hatred and affection, killing others and at the same time trying to find a peaceful life. It is shaped by the infinite activity of the past, always modifying itself. But the basic structure of reward and pain remains almost the same. This conditioning attempts to shape the outward world, but inwardly it is following the same pattern, always dividing the "me" and the "you", "we" and "they", being hurt and trying to hurt, a pattern in which passing affection and pleasure is the way of our life.

It is necessary to observe all this without value judgement if there is to be any deep, living change, to perceive the complexity of our life without choice, just to see exactly what is. What is is far more important than what should be. There is only what is and never what should be. What is can only end; it cannot become something else. The ending has greater significance than what is beyond ending. To search for what is beyond is to cultivate fear; to search for what lies beyond is to avoid, to turn away from what is. We are always chasing that which is not, something other than the actual. If we could see this and remain with what is, however unpleasant or fearful it may be, or however pleasurable, then observation, which is pure attention, dissipates that which is.

One of our difficulties is that we want to get on: one says to oneself, 'I understand this, then what?' The "what" is slipping away from what is. The "what" is the movement of thought. If something is painful, thought tries to avoid it, but if it is pleasurable, thought holds it and prolongs it. So this is one of the aspects of conflict.

There is no opposite, but only what actually is. As there is no opposite in the psychological sense, the observation of what is does not entail conflict. But our brains are conditioned to the illusion of the opposite. Of course there are opposites: light and dark, man and woman, black and white, tall and short, and so on, but here we are trying to study the psychological field of conflict. The ideal breeds conflict; and we are conditioned by centuries of idealism: the ideal State, the ideal man, the prototype, the god. It is this division between the prototype and the actual that breeds conflict. To see the truth of this is not a judgemental evaluation.

I have studied carefully what has been said in this letter. I understand the logic of it, the common sense of it, but the weight of the past is so heavy that the persistent, constant intrusion of cultivated illusion, of the ideal of what should be, is always interfering. I am asking myself whether this illusion can be totally dispelled, or if I should accept it as an illusion and let it wither away. I can see that the more I struggle against it, the more I am giving life to it, and it is very difficult to remain with what is. Now, as an educator, as both parent and teacher, can I convey this subtle and complex problem of conflict in human beings? What a wonderful life it would be without conflict, without problems. Or rather, as problems arise, which seems to be inevitable, to deal with them immediately and not live with them.

The way of education so far has been to cultivate competition and thereby sustain conflict. So I see one problem after another piling up in my responsibility to the student. The difficulties drown me, and so I begin to lose the vision of a good human being. I am using the word vision not as some ideal, not as a goal in the future, but as the actual deep reality of goodness and beauty. It is not some fanciful dream, a thing to be achieved; the very truth of it is a liberating factor. This perception is logical, reasonable and utterly sane. It has no overtones of sentimentality or romantic froth.

Now, I am faced with the total acceptance of what is, and I see my students caught in the avoidance of the actual. So there is a contradiction here; and if I am not careful and watchful in my relation with them, I will bring about conflict, a struggle between them and me. I see, but they do not, which is a fact. I want to help them to see. It is not my perception of truth, but for each one of them to see the truth which belongs to nobody. Any form of pressure is a distorting factor, as in giving or being an example, so I have to go at this very gently and interest them in investigating whether the ending of conflict is possible or not.

It has now taken me perhaps a week or more to understand this, to grasp the significance of it. I may not actually be living this, but I have grasped the delicate device of it, and it must not slip away from me. If they grasp even the perfume of this, it is as a living seed. I am discovering that patience has no element of time, whereas impatience is in the nature of time. I am not trying to achieve a result or come to a certain conclusion. I am not engulfed by all this; there is a regenerating factor.

50. CHOICE

Freedom has no opposite

Freedom is very necessary in our life. Freedom is obviously not to do whatever we like, though this has been considered freedom and has been the way of our life. We feel thwarted, inhibited when our desires are denied. From this arise our resentments, our feelings that we are set upon, and so a continuous revolt. We have followed this course of life and we can see, if we are at all thoughtful, that it has brought utter chaos to the world. Some psychologists have encouraged us to pursue our impulses without any restraint, to do what we like immediately, rationalizing such activity as necessary for each one's growth. This was actually the cry for many generations, though there was outward restraint, and now it is called "freedom" to allow the child to do what he wants up the ladder of his life, which is society. Perhaps, now, there will be an opposite swing toward control, inhibition, discipline and psychological restraint. This appears to be the story of mankind.

Added to this are the computer and the robot. The technology that is developing in this direction hopes to produce and probably will produce a computer with a human-like brain, but which may think faster and more accurately and thus give freedom from long hours of labour. The computer, too, is gradually taking over the education of our children: teachers and professors highly qualified in their various subjects can inform the students without actually being present. This, too, will give us a certain freedom.

Except in the totalitarian States, greater freedom is going to come to man and will perhaps allow him to do what he likes. Thus greater conflict may arise, greater misery and wars for man. When technology and computers with robots dominate and become part of our daily life, then what is to happen to the human brain, which has been active so far in outward physical struggle? Will the brain become atrophied when people work only a couple of hours or more? When relationship is between machine and machine, what is to happen to the quality and vitality of the brain? Will it seek some form of entertainment, religious or otherwise, or will it allow itself to explore the vast recesses of one's being? The industry of entertainment is gathering more and more strength, and very little human energy and capacity are turned inwardly; so, if we are not aware, the entertainment world is going to conquer us.

So we must ask what freedom is. It is often said that freedom is at the end of drastic discipline and civilized control – "civilized" meaning in the sense of having literature, art, museums and good food. This is merely the outward coating of a confused, declining human being. Is freedom to have a choice of entertainment? Is freedom choice at all? We always consider freedom as being from something, from bondage, anxiety, loneliness, despair, and so on. Such consideration leads only to further, and perhaps more refined, states of misery, sorrow and the ugliness of hatred. Freedom is not in choosing a political or religious leader to follow, which obviously denies freedom. Freedom is not the opposite of slavery. Freedom is an ending, not giving continuity to what has been. Freedom, in itself, has no opposite.

After having read this and studied it, what is my relationship not only to the student and to my wife and children, but to the world? Really to understand the depth of freedom, one needs a great deal of intelligence and perhaps love. But the activities of the world are not intelligent and neither is my group of children. I spend most of my day with them. Have I this quality of freedom with its intelligence and love? If I have this, my problems become very simple. That very quality will operate, and what I thought to be a problem will cease to be one. But I really do not have this. I can pretend, put on a show of friendliness, but that is very shallow. My responsibility is immediate. I cannot say to myself that I will wait until I achieve freedom and this affection, love. I literally have no time because my students are in front of me. I cannot become a hermit. That will not solve any problem, mine or the world's. I need lightning from heaven to have this freedom and love, to break up this incrustation, this conditioning; but there is no thunderbolt, no heaven. I can allow myself to come to an impasse and get depressed over the matter;

but it is an escape from the problem to completely enclose myself and thus be incapable of facing the actuality.

When I actually see the truth that there is no outside agent to help me in this dilemma, that no outside influence, no grace, no prayer will help in this matter, then perhaps I will have an uncontaminated energy. That energy may then be freedom and love.

But have I the energy of intelligence to dismantle the things that human beings all over the world, of whom I am one, have built psychologically around themselves? Have I the persistence to go through all this? I am asking these questions of myself, and I shall be asking them of my students in a more gentle and benevolent manner. I see the implications of all this quite clearly and I must tread very softly. The true answer lies in intelligence and love. If we have these qualities we will know what to do. We must realize the truth of this very deeply; otherwise we shall all be perpetuating in one form or another the confusion between human beings.

51. THE LIMITATION
OF KNOWLEDGE

We do not learn from wars
but repeat brutality and bestiality

Intelligence is not the consequence of discipline. It is not a by product of thought. Thought is the result of knowledge and ignorance. The discipline of thought, though it has certain values, leads to conformity. The way of discipline as it is generally understood is conformity, to imitate and follow a pattern. Discipline really means to learn, not to bow down to a standard. There can be no discipline without love.

From childhood we are told to mould ourselves according to a religious or social structure, to control ourselves, to obey. That discipline is based on reward and punishment. Discipline is inherent in every subject. If you want to be a good golfer or tennis player, it demands that you pay attention to every stroke, to respond quickly and gracefully; the very game has its own intrinsic natural order. This instructive order has gone out of our life, which has become chaotic, ruthless, competitive, and in which we seek power with all its pleasures.

Doesn't discipline imply learning the whole complex movement of life – social, personal and beyond the personal? Our life is fragmented, and we try to understand each fragment or integrate the fragments. If we recognize all this, the mere imposition of discipline and certain concepts becomes rather meaningless, but without some form of control most of us would go berserk. Certainly inhibitions hold us, compel us to follow tradition.

One realizes that there must be a certain order in our life. Is it possible to have order without any form of compulsion, without any pressure and, essentially, without reward or punishment? The social order is chaotic. There is injustice – the rich and poor, and so on. Every reformer tries to bring about social equality, and apparently not one of them has succeeded. Governments try to impose order by force, by law, by subtle propaganda. Though we may put a lid on all this, the pot is still boiling. So we must approach the problem differently. We have tried in every sort of way to civilize man, to tame him, and this, too, has not been very successful. Every war is barbarism, whether it is a holy war or a political war. So we must come back to the question: can there be order that is not the contrivance of thought?

Discipline means the art of learning. For most of us learning means storing up memory, reading a great many books, being able to quote from various authors, collecting words so as to write, speak or convey other people's ideas or our own, so as to act efficiently as an engineer or a scientist, a musician or a good mechanic. One may excel in the knowledge of these things, and thus make oneself more and more capable of having money, power and position. This is generally accepted as learning – to accumulate knowledge and to act from that; or, through action, to accumulate knowledge, which comes to the same. This has been our tradition, our custom, and so we are always living and learning in the field of the known. We are not suggesting there is something unknown, but to have an insight into the activities of the known, its limitations, its dangers and its endless continuity. The story of man is this. We do not learn from wars, we repeat wars; and brutality and bestiality continue with their corruption.

Only if we actually see the limitation of knowledge – that the more we pile up, the more barbarous we are becoming – can we begin to inquire into what is order that is not imposed externally or that is self-imposed, which both imply conformity and so endless conflict. Conflict is disorder. The apprehension of all this is attention, not concentration, and attention is the essence of intelligence and love. This naturally brings order without compulsion.

Now, as educators and as parents, which are the same, isn't it possible for us to convey this to our students and children? They may be too young to understand all that we have just read. We see the difficulties, and these very difficulties prevent us from grasping the greater issue. I am not making this into a problem; I am just very much aware of what chaos is and what order is. These two have no relation to each other. One is not born out of the other; and I am not denying one or accepting the other.

The flowering seed of perception will bring correct action.

52. HUMILITY

Humility is the essence of love and
intelligence; it is not an achievement

In every civilization there have been a few who were concerned and desirous of bringing about good human beings; a few who would not be involved in sacred structures or reform, but who would not harm another human being; who would be concerned with the whole of human life; who would be gentle, unaggressive and so would be truly religious. In modern civilization throughout the world, the cultivation of goodness has almost disappeared. The world is becoming more brutal, harmful, full of violence and deception. Surely it is our function as educators to bring about a quality of mind that is fundamentally religious. We do not mean belonging to some orthodox religion with its fantastic beliefs, its repetitive rituals. Man has always tried to find something beyond this world of anxiety, suffering and endless conflict. In his search for that which is not of the world, he has, probably unconsciously, invented God and many forms of divinity, and made interpreters between himself and that which he has projected. There have been many interpreters, highly sophisticated, talented, and learned. Historically from ancient times this cycle has continued – God, the interpreter and man. This is the real trinity in which human gullibility has been held. The world has been too much for us, and each human being wants some comfort, security and peace. So humans have projected the essence of all this into an outside agency, and that too we are discovering to be an illusion. Not being able to go beyond and above all the limitations of human struggle, we are returning to barbarism, destroying each other inwardly and outwardly.

As a small group can we begin to think about these things and, freeing ourselves from all the invented superstitions of religion, discover what a religious life is, and thus prepare the soil for the flowering of goodness? Without the religious mind there can be no goodness.

There are three factors in understanding the nature of religion: austerity, humility and diligence. Austerity does not mean reducing all of life to ashes by severe discipline, suppressing every instinct, every desire and even beauty. Outward expression of this suppression in the Asiatic world was the saffron robe and a loincloth; in the Western world it was becoming a monk and taking vows of celibacy and utter obedience. Simplicity of life may be expressed in outer garments and living a restricted life in a narrow cell, but inwardly the flame of desire burnt steadily and made for conflict. That flame was to be put out by strict adherence to a concept, to an image. The book and the image became the symbols of a simple life.

Austerity is not the outward expression of a conclusion based on faith, but to understand the inward complexity, the confusion and the agony of life. This understanding, which is not verbal or intellectual, requires a very careful, watchful perception, a perception that is not the complexity of thought, but is clarity. This clarity brings about its own austerity.

Humility is not the opposite of vanity, is not bowing one's head to some abstract authority or to the high priest. It is not the act of surrender to a guru or to an image, which are the same. It is not total denial and sacrificing oneself to some imaginary or physical being. Humility is not associated with arrogance. Humility has no sense of possessiveness inwardly. Humility is the essence of love and intelligence; it is not an achievement.

The other factor is diligence, which is for thought to be aware of its activities, its deceptions, its illusions. It is to discern the actual and the false that transforms the actual into "what should be". It is to be aware of reactions to the world outside and to the inner whispering responses. It is not self-centred watchfulness, but to be sensitive to all relationship.

Above and beyond all these are intelligence and love. When they exist, all the other qualities will follow. It is like opening the gate to beauty.

Now I come back as an educator and a parent to my stumbling question. My students and my children have to face the world, which is everything other than intelligence and love. This is not a cynical statement; it is palpable and evident. They have to face corruption, brutality and utter callousness. They are frightened. Being responsible – I am using that word very carefully, and with deep intention – how are we to help them to face all this? I am not asking the question of anyone else; I am putting it to myself so that in questioning I become clear. I am greatly troubled by this, and I certainly do not want a comforting answer. In questioning myself, sensitivity and clarity are showing their beginnings. I feel very strongly about the future of these students and children, and by helping them to use words, intelligence and love, I am gathering strength. To help one boy or one girl to be like this is sufficient for me, for the river begins in the high mountains as a very small stream, lonely and far away. But it gathers momentum into a huge river. So one must begin with the very few.

53. MEDIOCRITY

What energy will make us move
out of the commonplace?

What we are the world is. In the family, in society, we have made this world with its vulgarity, brutality, cruelty and coarseness and destroy each other. We also destroy each other psychologically, exploiting one another for our desires and gratification. We never seem to realize that unless each one of us undergoes a radical change, the world will continue as it has for thousands of years, with us maiming each other, killing each other and despoiling the earth. If our own house is not in order, we cannot possibly expect society and our relationships to one another to be in order. It is all so obvious that we neglect it. We discard it as being not only simple but too arduous, so we accept things as they are, fall into the habit of acceptance, and carry on. This is the essence of mediocrity. One may have a literary gift, be recognized by the few, and work towards popularity; one may be a painter, a poet or a great musician; but in our daily lives we are not concerned with the whole of existence. We may perhaps be adding to the great confusion and misery of mankind. Each one wants to express his own little talent and be satisfied with it, forgetting or neglecting the whole complexity of man's trouble and sorrow. We accept this, and it has become the normal way of life. We are never an outsider and remain outside; we feel ourselves incapable of remaining outside, or are afraid not to be in the current of the commonplace.

As parents and educators, we make the family and the school what we are. Mediocrity really means going only half-way up the mountain and never reaching the top. We want to be like everybody else, or if we want to be slightly different, we keep it carefully hidden. We are not talking of eccentricity, which is another form of self-expression, which is what everyone is doing in his own little way. Eccentricity is only tolerated if you are well-to-do or gifted, but if you are poor and act peculiarly, you are snubbed and ignored. But few of us are talented; we are workers carrying on with our particular professions.

The world is becoming more and more mediocre. Our education, our occupation, our superficial acceptance of traditional religion are making us mediocre and rather sloppy. We are concerned here with our daily life, not with the expression of talent or some capacity. As educators, which includes parents, can we break away from this plodding, mechanical way of living? Is it the unconscious fear of loneliness that makes us fall into habits – the habit of work, the habit of thought, the habit of general acceptance of things as they are? We establish a routine for ourselves and live as closely as possible to that habit, so gradually the brain becomes mechanical. This mechanical way of living is mediocrity. The countries that live on established traditions are generally mediocre. So we are asking ourselves in what way can mechanical mediocrity end and not form another pattern which will gradually become mediocre too?

The mechanical use of thought is the issue, not how to step out of mediocrity, but that man has given complete importance to thought. All our activities and aspirations, our relationships and longings are based on thought. Thought is common to all, whether they are highly talented or villagers without any kind of education. Thought is common to all of us. It is neither of the East nor of the West, the lowlands or the highlands. It is not yours or mine. This is important to understand. We have made it personal and, by doing so, have further limited the nature of thought. Thought is limited, but when we make it our own we make it still shallower. When we see the truth of this, there will be no competition between the thought of ideals and everyday thought. The ideal has become all-important and not the thought of action. It is this division that breeds conflict, and to accept conflict is mediocre. It is the politicians and the gurus who nourish and sustain this conflict and so mediocrity.

Again we come to the basic issue: what is the response of the teacher and the parent, which includes all of us, to the coming generation? We may perceive the logic and the sanity of what is said in these letters, but the intellectual comprehension does not seem to give us the vital energy to propel us out of our mediocrity. What is that energy which will make us move – now, not eventually – out of the commonplace? Surely it is not enthusiasm or the sentimental grasp of some vague perception, but is an energy that sustains itself under all circumstances. What is that energy, which must be independent of all outside influence? This is a serious question each is asking himself. Is there such energy, totally free from all causation?

Now let us examine it together. Thought is the outcome of cause which is knowledge. That which has a dimension always has an end. When we say we understand, it generally means an intellectual or verbal comprehension, but comprehending is to perceive sensitively that which is, and that very perception is the withering away of that which is. Perception is this attention that is focussing all energy to watch the movement of that which is. This energy of perception has no cause, as intelligence and love have no cause.

54. HARMONY WITH NATURE

If you hurt nature
you are hurting yourself

Surely educators are aware of what is actually happening in the world. People are divided racially, religiously, politically, economically, and this division is fragmentation. It is bringing about great chaos in the world – wars, every kind of deception politically, and so on. There is the spreading violence of man against man. This is the actual state of confusion in the world, in the society in which we live; and this society is created by all human beings with their culture, their linguistic divisions, their regional separations. All this is breeding not only confusion but hatred, a great deal of antagonism and further linguistic differences.

This is what is happening; and the responsibility of the educator is really very great. He is concerned in all these schools to bring about a good human being who has a feeling of global relationship, who is not nationalistic, regional, separate, religiously clinging to the old, dead traditions, which really have no value at all. The responsibility of the educator becomes more and more serious, more and more committed, more and more concerned with the education of his students.

What is education doing actually? Is it really helping mankind, our children, to become more concerned, more gentle, generous, not to go back to the old pattern, the old ugliness and naughtiness of this world? If the educator is really concerned, as he must be, then he has to help the student to find out his relationship to the world, not to the world of imagination or romantic sentimentality, but to the actual world in which all things are taking place; and also to the world of nature, to the desert, the jungle or the few trees that surround him, and to the animals of the world. (Animals, fortunately, are not nationalistic; they hunt only to survive.) If the educator and the student lose their relationship to nature, to the trees, to the rolling sea, each will certainly lose his relationship with humanity.

What is nature? There is a great deal of talk about and endeavour to protect nature, the animals, the birds, the whales and dolphins, to clean the polluted rivers, the lakes, the green fields, and so on. Nature is not put together by thought, as religion is, as belief is. Nature is the tiger, that extraordinary animal with its energy, its great sense of power. Nature is the solitary tree in the field, the meadows and the grove; it is that squirrel shyly hiding behind a bough. Nature is the ant and the bee and all the living things of the earth. Nature is the river, not a particular river, whether the Ganges, the Thames or the Mississippi. Nature is all those mountains, snow clad, with dark blue valleys and ranges of hills meeting the seas. The universe is part of this world. One must have a feeling for all this, not destroy it, not kill for one's pleasure, not kill animals for food. We do kill the vegetables that we eat, but one must draw the line somewhere. If you do not eat vegetables, then how will you live? So one must intelligently discern.

Nature is part of our life. We grew out of the seed, the earth, and we are part of all that, but we are rapidly losing the sense that we are animals like the others. Can you have a feeling for a tree, look at it, see the beauty of it, listen to the sound it makes; be sensitive to the little plant, to the little weed, to the creeper that is growing up the wall, to the light on the leaves and the many shadows? You must be aware of all this and have that sense of communion with nature around you. You may live in a town, but you do have trees here and there. The next-door garden may be ill-kept, crowded with weeds, but look at the flower in it, and feel that you are part of all that, part of all living things. If you hurt nature you are hurting yourself.

One knows that all this has been said before in different ways, but we don't seem to pay much attention. Is it that we are so caught up in our own network of problems, our own desires, our own urges of pleasure and pain that we never look around, never watch the moon? Watch it. Watch with all your eyes and ears, your sense of smell. Watch. Look as though you are looking for the first time. If you can do that, you are seeing the tree, the bush, the blade of grass for the first time. Then you can see your teacher, your mother and father, your brother and sister, for the first time. There is an extraordinary feeling about that, like the wonder, the strangeness, the miracle of a fresh morning that has never been before, never will be again.

Be really in communion with nature, not verbally caught in the description of it, but be a part of it, be aware, feel that you belong to all that. Be able to have love for all that, to admire a deer, the lizard on the wall, a broken branch lying on the ground. Look at the evening star or the new moon, without the word, without merely saying how beautiful it is and turning your back on it, attracted by something else. Watch that single star and new delicate moon as though for the first time. If there is such communion between you and nature, then you can commune with man, with the student sitting next to you, with your educator, or with your parents. We have lost all sense of relationship in which there is not only a verbal statement of affection and concern but also this sense of communion which is not verbal. It is a sense that we are all together, that we are all human beings, not divided, not broken up, not belonging to any particular group or race, or to some idealistic concepts, but that we are all human beings and we are all living on this extraordinary, beautiful earth.

Have you ever woken up in the morning and looked out of the window, or gone out and looked at the trees and the spring dawn? Live with it. Listen to all the sounds, to the whisper, the slight breeze among the leaves. See the light on a leaf and watch the sun coming over the hill, over the meadow; and the dry river, or sheep grazing across the hill. Watch them; look at them with a sense of affection, care, that you do not want to hurt a thing. When you have such communion with nature, then your relationship with another person becomes simple, clear, without conflict.

This is one of the responsibilities of the educator, not merely to teach mathematics or how to use a computer. It is far more important to have communion with other human beings who suffer, struggle and have great pain and the sorrow of poverty – and also with the rich people who go by in a car. If the educator is concerned with this, he is helping the student to become sensitive to other people's sorrows, other people's struggles, anxieties and worries, and the rows that one has in the family. It should be the responsibility of the teacher to educate the children, the students, to have such communion with the world. The world may be too large, but the world is where he is; that is his world. And this brings about a natural consideration, affection for others, courtesy and behaviour that is not rough, cruel, vulgar.

The educator should talk about all these things – not just verbally; he must feel the world, the world of nature and the world of man. They are interrelated. Man cannot escape from that. When he destroys nature, he is destroying himself. When he kills another, he is killing himself. The enemy is not the other but you. To live in such harmony with nature, with the world, naturally brings about a different world.

55. THERE IS ONLY LEARNING

Learning brings about equality
among human beings

By watching, perhaps you learn more than from books. Books are necessary to learn a subject, whether it is mathematics, geography, history, physics or chemistry. Books have printed on a page the accumulated knowledge of scientists, of philosophers, of archaeologists, and so on. This accumulated knowledge, which one learns in school and then through college or university, if one is lucky enough to go to university, has been gathered through the ages, from very ancient days. There is great accumulated knowledge from India, from ancient Egypt, Mesopotamia, the Greeks, the Romans and of course the Persians. In the Western world as well as in the Eastern world this knowledge is necessary to have a career, to do any job, whether mechanical or theoretical, practical or something that you have to think out, invent. This knowledge has brought about a great deal of technology, especially in the twentieth century. There is knowledge of the so-called sacred books, the Vedas, the Upanishads, the Bible, the Koran and the Hebrew Scriptures. There are the religious books and pragmatic books, books that will help you to have knowledge, to act skilfully, whether you are an engineer, a biologist or a carpenter.

Most of us in any school, and particularly in these schools, gather knowledge, information. That is what schools have existed for so far, to gather a great deal of information about the world outside, about the heavens, why the sea is salty, why the trees grow, about human beings, their anatomy, the structure of the brain, and so on, and also about the world around you, nature, the social environment, economics, and so much else. Such knowledge is absolutely necessary, but knowledge is always limited. However much it may evolve, the gathering of knowledge is always limited. Learning is part of acquiring this knowledge of various subjects so that you can have a career, a job that might please you, or one that circumstances, social demands may force you to accept, though you may not like very much to do that kind of work.

As we have said, you learn a great deal by watching – watching the things about you, watching the birds, the trees, watching the heavens, the stars, the constellation of Orion, the Dipper, the Evening Star. You learn just by watching not only the things around you but also by watching people, how they walk, their gestures, the words they use, how they are dressed. You watch not only what is outside you but you also watch yourself, why you think this or that, your behaviour, the conduct of your daily life, why parents want you to do this or that. You are watching, not resisting. If you resist you don't learn. Or if you come to some kind of conclusion, some opinion you think is right and hold on to that, then naturally you will never learn. Freedom is necessary to learn, and curiosity, a sense of wanting to know why you or others behave in a certain way, why people are angry, why you get annoyed.

Learning is extraordinarily important, because learning is endless. Learning why human beings kill each other, for instance. Of course there are explanations in books, all the psychological reasons why human beings behave in their particular ways, why human beings are violent. All this has been explained in books of various kinds by eminent authors, psychologists, and so on. But what you read is not what you are. If you watch yourself, what you are, how you behave, why you get angry, envious, why you get depressed, you learn much more than from a book that tells you what you are. But it is easier to read a book about yourself than to watch yourself. The brain is accustomed to gather all its information from external actions and reactions. Don't you find it much more comforting to be directed, for others to tell you what you should do? Your parents, especially in the East, tell you whom you should marry and arrange the marriage, tell you what your career should be. So the brain accepts the easy way, and the easy way is not always the right way.

I wonder if you have noticed that nobody loves their work anymore, except perhaps a few scientists, artists, archaeologists. But the ordinary, average person seldom loves what he is doing. He is compelled by society, by his parents or by the urge to have more money. So learn by watching very, very carefully the external world, the world outside you, and also the inner world; that is, the world of yourself.

There appear to be two ways of learning. One is acquiring a great deal of knowledge, first through study, and then by acting from that knowledge. That is what most of us do. The second is to act, to do something and learn through doing; and that also becomes the accumulation of knowledge. Really both are the same – learning from a book or acquiring knowledge through action. Both are based upon knowledge, experience; and as we have said, experience and knowledge are always limited.

So both the educator and the student should find out what learning actually is. For example, you may learn from a guru if he is at all the right kind – a sane guru, not the moneymaking guru, not one of those who want to be famous and trot off to different countries to gather a fortune through their rather unbalanced theories. Find out what it is to learn. Today learning is becoming more and more a form of entertainment. In some Western schools when the students have passed high school, secondary school, they do not even know how to read and write; and when you do know how to read and write, and learn various subjects, you are all such mediocre people. Do you know what the word mediocrity means? The root meaning is to go half way up the hill, never reaching the top. That is mediocrity, never demanding the excellent, the very highest thing of yourself. And learning is infinite, it really has no end.

So from whom are you learning? From books? From the educator? Perhaps, if your mind is bright, by watching? So far, it appears you are learning from the outside. You are learning, accumulating knowledge, and acting from that knowledge, establishing your career, and so on. If you are learning from yourself, or rather if you are learning by watching yourself, your prejudices, your definite conclusions, your beliefs, if you are watching the subtleties of your thought, your vulgarity, your sensitivity, then you yourself become the teacher and the taught. Then you do not depend inwardly on anybody, not on any book, not on the specialist. If you are ill and have some sort of disease, of course you have to go to a specialist; that is natural, that is necessary. But to depend on somebody, however excellent he may be, prevents you from learning about yourself and what you are. And it is very, very important to learn what you are, because what you are brings about this society which is so corrupt, immoral; in which there is such enormous spreading of violence; this society which is so aggressive, each one seeking his own particular success, his own form of fulfilment. Learn what you are, not through another but by watching yourself; not condemning, not saying 'This is all right, I am that, I can't change', and carrying on. When you watch yourself without any form of reaction, resistance, then that very watching acts. Like a flame it burns away the stupidities, the illusions that one has.

So learning is important. A brain that ceases to learn becomes mechanical. It is like an animal tied to a stake; it can move only according to the length of the rope, the tether that is tied to the stake. Most of us are tied to a peculiar stake of our own, an invisible stake and rope. You keep wandering within the dimensions of that rope, and it is very limited. It is like a man who is thinking about himself all day, about his problems, his desires, his pleasures and what he would like to do. You know this constant occupation with oneself. It is very, very limited, and that very limitation breeds various forms of conflict and unhappiness.

The great poets, painters, composers are never satisfied with what they have done. They are always learning. You don't stop learning after you have passed your exams and gone to work. There is a great strength and vitality in learning, especially about yourself. Learn, watch so that there is no spot that is not uncovered, looked at in yourself. This really is to be free from your own particular conditioning. The world is divided through its conditioning as Indian, American, British, Russian, Chinese, and so on. Out of this conditioning there are wars, the killing of thousands of people, unhappiness and brutality.

So both the educator and the educated are learning in the deeper sense of that word. When both are learning there is no educator or the one to be educated: there is only learning. Learning frees the brain and thought from prestige, position, status. Learning brings about equality among human beings.

* * *

56. TRADITION

Revolt against the past
brings only another conformity

One of the most important things that all of us have to understand is the tremendous weight of tradition, especially in this country [India] where it is looked upon as a most sacred thing. The word tradition means to surrender, to deliver. When one surrenders oneself to the past, the mind is shaped or conditioned by that which has been. The past then becomes tremendously important, in contrast, in opposition, to the present.

The past is cultivated through rituals, through the so-called sacred books, through religious propaganda. This conditions the mind and so limits it. In that limitation the traditionalist seeks freedom. This is like a prisoner who extends the walls of his prison: he is still in prison however large the yard he walks in. These customs that have been so carefully cultivated by past generations are handed down through the family, through literature, through environmental influences; what matters is not the culture of the mind, but rather to control the mind by patterns established in the past, which it is hoped will bring about order. That is the purpose of tradition.

Against this weight of tradition all the young generations, from Socrates down, have rebelled – the hippies, the beatniks and others, with their uniforms of long hair, beards, and so on. This revolt against the past brings about only another type of conformity, and it indicates, doesn't it, a great protest against the established order of things and against the past generation, which is responsible for wars, for the disorders in society, for the division of mankind into nationalities and religious groups?

Freedom from the past is not revolt against the past, but rather the understanding of how the past – tradition, custom – has shaped our minds and hearts. In studying this conditioning, which is critical awareness of oneself, in seeing oneself as a prisoner in this world of great sorrow which one has created, comes freedom. Without this freedom you cannot possibly act in the present. The active present is the only action.

Either you are going to repudiate the past completely or you are going to be swallowed up by society, which is to surrender to society, to deliver yourself over to society, with its traditions, with its wars, and so on. That is, you will become the established order for your children, who will revolt against you if they are at all intelligent. The revolt of the young has been going on for thousands of years. Each generation destroys the young through wrong education and ideologies that have no value at all. To break this chain is the major purpose of education, not just to cultivate a strong memory which will function to help earn a livelihood. Right education is to help the student not merely to pass examinations in technical subjects, but to understand the whole field of existence, which is your life. Not only the educator but also the student must demand this kind of education; and through questioning, through discussions, through the general assembly of the school in which the relationship between the educator and the student is not one of authority, they must see that this education is maintained.

In tradition no goodness can flower, and the continuity of tradition is not goodness.

57. CULTURE

True culture is a movement in freedom

Culture, as the word indicates, is something that is constantly growing, changing, a movement without any particular end. To cultivate a plant or a flower, it needs attention and protection, and to cultivate the mind is much more difficult. The mind is very complex, very subtle, and has immense possibilities that are really incalculable. We neglect the totality of the mind and try to cultivate a very small part of it through education, through learning a technique which will give us the capacity to earn a livelihood. This particular little training that one gets through education, through social contacts, through relationship with other human beings leads to contradiction, which is expressed in daily life in conflict, hatred, antagonism, and the competitive aggression which has become so important merely to survive. And because one is not able to bring about an end to this contradiction in oneself and in the society or the community in which one lives, one escapes to temples, to churches or mosques, to drink or to exaggerated sexual relationships, and so on. All escapes are essentially the same, whether they are escapes to so-called God or through giving importance to sex.

The cultivation of the fragment must inevitably lead to destruction and sorrow, whether that fragment is the nation, a particular belief, the family, or an idea. Cultivation of the glory and the success of the fragment must divide, separate, and so bring about chaos in the world. Till now the cultivation of the fragment has been the main concern of education, of society. This fragmentary cultivation must nurture fear and so the constant search for security, both outer and inner. This is the society in which we live, with its wars, violence, brutality, aggression, and the ever-mounting sorrow.

In a school, if we give all importance to acquiring technical knowledge and totally neglect the vastness of the mind as human beings, we shall become mechanical, bored with life, and fundamentally lazy. This is what is taking place. You can cultivate the fragment, but you cannot cultivate the whole field because you do not have the instrument with which to enter this vastness. We do not realize this, and so the intellect becomes all-important, or we give an emotional, enthusiastic devotion to a particular ideology – of the State, or of one's own image, or of a concept of this vastness which is called religion. Something cultivated by man in his fears becomes tradition.

So our problem is not only to have first-class training in technological knowledge, but also to feel our way into this extraordinary mind, with all its immensity. You will inevitably ask how this is to be done. The "how" is the method, the system, and if you follow the system or the method, it doesn't matter what it is, whose it is, you are again cultivating the fragment. When you realize this you will not ask how.

So you have already plunged into a different investigation. This investigation demands complete freedom. This freedom is not disorder; it is not laisser-aller. If you have ever demanded this freedom of yourself, you have also built an image, a concept, an idea of what this freedom is, and obviously that is not freedom. Freedom is not something to be found in heaven but in our daily lives, in freedom from brutality, violence, greed, and so on. Without this foundation of freedom, the growth of the fragment brings chaos and untold mischief and misery.

True culture is a movement in freedom, not within the pattern of an ideology, which becomes tradition.

58. OBEDIENCE

Fear breeds authority

One of the most important things in life, perhaps the most important, is freedom. This word has been greatly misused by tyrannical as well as democratic governments, and religions everywhere in the world have abused it. Personal freedom and independence do not exist, except perhaps in the scientific world. It does not exist in the business world or in the religious structures which man has organized through fear and belief; it does not exist in governments or in any field of human activity. But man has consistently asserted that he is free and complained that it is environment that enslaves him. Freedom, which is independence to think for oneself clearly and not to act according to the dictates of society or one's own personal inclinations, is very difficult, but without freedom one cannot possibly discover or live a life which is totally different from the misery which we all know every day.

Freedom is not merely freedom from something, but is freedom in itself. This does not mean freedom to do whatever one likes, so one has to understand not merely verbally but factually what that word implies. We are not trying to define what freedom is; each one would interpret it according to his own fancy, inclination or upbringing, and some would even deny that there is such a thing at all. Freedom is to be found not by seeking it, but rather by understanding what it is that imprisons the mind. When these prison walls are broken, then there is freedom naturally, and one does not have to seek it. So what is important is not how to achieve freedom or to ask what freedom is, but rather to ask why the mind – which is the product of time and environment and has had so many experiences of misery and conflict – is not free.

What is important is to inquire into why the mind still remains so heavily conditioned after so many millions of years. This is the prison in which it lives. The mind is conditioned by society with its cultures, laws, religious sanctions, economic pressures, and so on.

The mind is, after all, the result of the past, and this past is tradition. It lives in this tradition with all its strife, wars and agonies. One must ask if it can be free from its own conditioning. Some have said that it must always remain conditioned and can never be free, and others have said this freedom from conditioning can never be found here but only in some future heaven, or at the end of some long sacrifice, discipline, programme of further conformity to a pattern of so-called religious practice. Without freedom from conditioning, humanity will always remain a prisoner and life will remain a battlefield.

The first thing to understand in this inquiry is the nature of authority. In any community, law and the policeman are necessary, but we have also introduced a policeman into the inner world of thought and feeling. In this world, obedience has been instilled by tradition, experience and habit – obedience to one's parents, to society, to the priest. But obedience is born of fear – fear of going wrong, of acting independently, of not being secure, of not being part of the community, of standing alone, of making a mistake. So it is fear that breeds authority; one wants to live in a respected, accepted way which society has established. It is this very fear that has conditioned the mind; it is fear that has built the society to which the mind has become a slave. The mind has created this society through its fear, greed, ambition, envy, and so on.

A discipline which comes naturally, without any conformity, is the simple observation of all these fears, anxieties, and envies; to see your own fears, your own ambitions as you see a tree. This very seeing is that discipline. The word discipline means learning, not conformity, suppression or obedience. Learning about the nature and structure of conditioning brings order, not the order of society which is disorder.

So, seeing what the world is, with its wars, hatred, strife, confusions, is to see yourself as you are. And to see yourself as you are is to see the world which you have created from what you are. In this seeing is freedom. To see a danger is to avoid it. To see the danger of this heavy conditioning of man is to avoid all conditioning. What is important in all this is to see not only with the intellect but also with the actual eye.

59. CONFLICT

Separation leads to conflict

To avoid the world is to be worldly. We avoid it in so many ways. Avoidance is resistance to what is. The idealist and the intellectual, the emotional man, the religious man and the man of the world, all resist what is in their own specialized ways. So there is never any radical change or revolution. This resistance or avoidance is cultivated from childhood until we die. This has been the tradition not only in the East but also in the West; it does not belong to the East or the West, for man is not European, Asian or American. The fundamental question is whether it is possible to live a daily life without any resistance, that is, without any defence. Is it possible to be vulnerable, therefore highly sensitive, and yet carry on with our daily occupations?

As this is not done, the inevitable consequence is the separative process which one cultivates through the defence mechanism, and this separative process must inevitably lead to conflict in all relationships. This inner conflict becomes outer conflict leading to national divisions, religious divisions, moral divisions, and so on. Is it possible in society to live a life without conflict, without resistance, without any form of avoidance of what is? The what is is always in the active present. Resistance to this living activity comes through past memories of what has been and the hope of what might be. The remembrance of the past and the hope of the future is the avoidance of what is. We resist the actual. The actual is anger, or sorrow, or despair, or a moment of joy. Can one look at sorrow without any form of resistance or avoidance, look at it not only with the senses but also without the self-pitying process, and not escape from it, neither condemning it nor accepting it, which are both forms of avoiding what is? What is is sorrow or pain.

Looking is always in the present. If you say, 'I have looked', and you look at the present with what you have learnt from that look and with the memory of that look, then you are really looking with eyes that are clouded by past memories, and so you do not look at all. Really to look at this sorrow, with which humanity has lived since we began, is to look without time. When there is no resistance, then this sorrow loses its sting. But to accept sorrow, or to worship it, or to explain it away, is never to come into direct contact with it.

The network of escapes which we have cultivated through alcohol, through sex, through the organized beliefs we call religion, through obedience to the State or to some ideology, is in effect resistance to, avoidance of what is, both inwardly and outwardly. All cultivation of the tradition of resistance denies freedom. The remembrance of past action is inaction, for action is a movement in the present, the action which springs from what is, not from the remembrance of what was.

60. WORKING TOGETHER

Education is to break down patterns

Cooperation and aggression can never go together. Cooperation is an absolute necessity in a world which is so splintered by national and religious beliefs, economic differences and intellectual over- and underdevelopment. There is a certain kind of cooperation in very close relationships, as in the family, but beyond that there are always differences of opinion, inclinations and knowledge. These differences become intensified through ambition and envy, and this obviously prevents cooperation.

Traditionally, cooperation meant working together for an ideology or around a dominant individual or for some utopian ideal, but such cooperation ceases or disintegrates when the individual or the ideology disappears. This is the pattern man has followed, hoping to bring about a different condition in the world, or for his own personal profit. Working together for an end, with each individual having his own motive for the achievement of that end, must inevitably breed conflict. Such working together is for a concept and not a factual necessity. Working together ceases to be a formula when there is not only understanding of the necessity but also when there is that relationship which comes with love. This relationship is denied when there is aggression. Man, by nature, is aggressive; this aggression comes from the animal. This aggressiveness, this violence, is encouraged in the family, in education, in the business world and in religious structures.

Aggression takes the form of ambition, which again is encouraged and respected. Aggression is violence, and to counteract this violence which is so prominent in the world, various forms of ideology have been developed; but this only helps to avoid the actual fact of violence. Violence is not only on the battlefield but it is anger, hate and envy. It is the envy that makes us competitive, which again is a very highly respected thing in society, the very structure of which is based on violence.

Most of us can see the pattern of all this at least intellectually, but what makes us act is not an intellectual grasp but seeing the very truth of the matter. Seeing the truth is the only liberating factor, not all the intellectual arguments, the emotional adjustments or mere rationalizations. To see is to act, and that action is not the outcome of ideation.

Cooperation must exist, and it cannot possibly exist when each individual is in competition with other human beings and is pursuing his own fulfilment. In order to cooperate there can be no such thing as individual, family or national fulfilment, for this fulfilment emphasizes separation, denying cooperation. When you see all this, not as a descriptive idea but as a danger to the total well-being of mankind, then that very seeing brings an action that will be non-aggressive and so cooperative. To see is to love and a man who loves is in a state of cooperation. Understanding cooperation, he will also see when not to cooperate.

In the fullness of cooperation, goodness, which is not sentimentality, can flower. It is authority that destroys cooperation, for love cannot possibly exist where there is authority. We have lived so long in the accepted patterns of life that it has become traditional, and freedom, love and cooperation have lost their fundamental meanings. Education is to break down these patterns. In the very breaking down of them is the seeing of the truth of the new.

61. ORDER

Obedience to the past is disorder

Except perhaps in nature, when you look around you see that there is much misery, confusion and violence. If man had set out deliberately to bring about chaos in the world he could not possibly have succeeded as much as the present actual state of destruction, hatred and anarchy. This is the result of past generations; the lives, the attitudes, the values and the superstitions of the past generations are responsible for this chaos.

You often hear that the future is in the hands of the younger generation. Is this so? Or is it that the younger generations are also so heavily conditioned by the past – of which they may not be conscious at all – that they revolt only superficially against the established order? This superficial revolt gives them a certain vitality and freshness, which is mistaken for a new beginning. Every generation has been more or less in revolt against the past, but they are soon trapped by the past, by the society, culture in which they have lived. All this is fairly obvious and does not require deep analysis.

What is more urgent is that, as human beings, everyone of us has to think, act and live in a totally different way that is not based on aggression, acquisitiveness and the predatory instinct that man has inherited. This revolution is not in the social or the economic field but at a much greater depth; it is in the very structure of human consciousness. So the crisis is not one of youth against former generations, or one religious formula against another, or one country against another, but at the very roots of our being. The decision is whether we continue with the past or find a way of living in which conflict in any form does not exist.

To find a new way of life, order is necessary. Order is not imitation or acceptance of a pattern as a way of life. It is not obedience to a higher authority, whether that authority is outer or inner. Order is not conformity either to a way of life established through tradition or to a way of life cultivated for oneself. All such order is essentially a form of acceptance of conformity. Order cannot possibly exist when there is fear; fear and disorder go together. The social structure in which we live by its very nature produces this disorder. It is this disorder that we are frightened of, and we cultivate a morality to overcome this fear. So our so-called morality is no more than adjustment to disorder.

When we talk of order we mean a state of mind that is the natural outcome of understanding the actual nature of disorder. It is not the cultivation of a new pattern or system to be followed, but rather it is seeing the nature of disorder and its danger. If you cling to the old way of life, obviously you will not see the danger of this disorder. So the seeing of disorder is the discipline and not the other way round. Freedom does not come from discipline as it is generally understood, which is to conform, to suppress, to obey, and so on. Discipline means learning. So you have to become a disciple of freedom; and there is no guru or teacher to tell you what freedom is. So order is possible only when there is learning about freedom. This learning is the continuation of freedom in action.

So authority comes to an end. Of course there must be the authority of the policeman and the law, but there is no other authority. For freedom, which is order, cannot exist in the shadow of authority, whether it is the authority of tradition or the authority that one has gathered through experience and knowledge. Authority is always the past, and obedience to the past is disorder.

62. MORALITY

Conformity denies virtue

Tyrannical governments and tyrannical parents have tried to establish order through fear and punishment. They assume the authority of "Providence" itself to dominate and shape minds according to their concepts and traditions of what order should be. Tradition can be ten thousand years or one day old. In the family this authority is vested in the parents, and in tyrannical governments it is enforced through various forms of persuasion, murder and intimidation. Once they have established themselves in power, it is a simple matter for governments through propaganda to build a tradition that is gradually accepted to assure the continuation of their authority. The family, the church and tyrannical governments have done this throughout the ages. In this the basic law is acceptance, obedience and conformity, a conformity which both the tyrant and the parent consider will bring about order. Order for them means obeying what they consider to be the highest good for the community as well as the individual.

This so-called order tries to establish the relationship among individuals and between the individual and the community. This relationship is conditioned, but since all life is relationship, to force it into a particular mould must naturally bring about conflict. This conflict is revolt against the pattern, which brings about disorder; and to overcome this disorder, authority is again exercised to bring about so-called order. This obvious pattern can be seen working in the daily life of governments, religious organizations and all established power. This is not order at all.

Order must come out of freedom, not order first and freedom afterwards. Freedom cannot possibly exist if there is no discipline; but discipline according to the pattern of power or according to an established tradition or conformity to necessity is not discipline at all. As we have said, discipline is learning. Learning needs an active mind, not a mind that has accumulated knowledge and adds to it through what it calls learning. Learning demands attention; but it is inattention that is encouraged through the accumulation of knowledge and habit. Habit and knowledge are contrary to virtue. It is virtue that brings about order. Morality is custom and habit, and virtue is not. When we understand the mechanism of habit and custom – not intellectually but actually come directly into contact with it – then the very seeing is the liberating factor from custom and habit, which is the deep-rooted tradition that human beings have sedulously guarded and which is acceptance of tyranny and of the morality, the established order, of society.

So in all human beings there is this compulsive urge to conform, to follow, which is the very denial of virtue. Virtue as conduct, behaviour, can only flower as goodness when morality as custom ceases. So order is not custom compelled by authority, whether outer or inner, but the flowering of behaviour that is not shaped by the environment. Such behaviour is righteousness. Without righteous behaviour there is no order. We are so used to disorder, the indication of which is conflict, that to be without that mould brings fear. Fear only breeds resistance and aggression, and never order.

Love is not remembrance of the image of pleasure or desire, for this breeds contradiction and conflict, which is one of the causes of disorder. Love is not the photo on the mantelpiece or the image in the church or the sexual remembrance, which breed habit, custom and therefore disorder. Love is righteousness, behaviour in the active present, and this is order.

63. ACTION

Living is action in relationship

Surely we all seek a way of life in which conflict has no place. Humanity has sought this in a monastery, has become a wandering monk or has withdrawn from the world into a cave, an ivory tower, hoping to find a way of life in which pain and sorrow have come to an end. But mankind has accepted war, inwardly and outwardly, as a way of life. Even the monk goes through various struggles, chaos and anxieties. We have accepted life as a battlefield in which we are not only against each other but are also divided within the limited consciousness of our own being. So we only know a way of living which is turmoil and an action which brings more anxieties and despairs.

Now we can ask whether there is any action at all that does not breed conflict. Action is not an ideological concept of what action should be. Action is the very doing in the present. Action is never what has been or what will be. What has been is the memory of action, and what will be is the projection through the present of what has been. We think out an action and carry it out in the present, modifying it if necessary; so action is something which has been worked out by thought in the past for us. Action, therefore, is never in the present; it is always in the shadow of the past. This shadow is memory, experience and knowledge, an ideology or a concept of what action should be. And so action never is.

This division of action as the past in the present to produce a result in the future is the work of thought. Thought is the outcome of the past and so thought is always old. There is nothing new in thought, so when thought dominates action it ceases to be action but is only a result, an effect. But living, feeling, relationship are always in the present, the present being the active movement. So there is always a contradiction between what is and what has been, and so this action always produces conflict.

When one sees this whole structure of what we call action, with its resultant conflicts, one asks oneself whether action can spring not out of thought but out of a state of mind that is utterly quiet and silent. Only then can action be not a result, and so not productive of pain and sorrow.

The emptying of the mind of the past is meditation; and then action is meditation. After all, living is action in relationship. For the mind to free itself from the image of the past is the action of meditation.

64. PREJUDICE

Relationship is not intellectual

Violence and nihilism are spreading throughout the world. The more highly organized society is, the more possibility there is of violence; and the sense of non-cooperation, which is nihilism, must be on the increase. Law cannot solve this problem for we all depend on each other. If one highly specialized group strikes against another and the strike is legal, there is no way out of this disorder. The tyrannical States have forbidden strikes, but that is not the way either. Each specialized segment of the community is opposing another specialized group; and the poor, seeing affluence, naturally want part of it.

So there is tremendous struggle going on within society, leading to violence in every form. Law and police order cannot bring peace to the world, and we must have peace to survive at all. Peace is not established by the politicians; theirs is only a peace between two conflicts. Peace is in the relationship of human beings whether they are black, white or pink, communist or Catholic, and so on. The relationship is not at the intellectual level. A relationship at that level is no relationship at all. Relationship is on the human level of understanding and affection. This is denied when action conforms or adjusts to an image made by the intellect. Ideas are far more important to us than the human relationship of affection with its consideration.

Why have formulas become so important? Is it because we do not know how to act, and so escape into ideas, into formulas with which we hope to solve the problems? To kill an animal or a human being is the ultimate act of violence. We all recognize this deep down in our hearts, but yet find reasons, logical and illogical, why we should kill. So killing becomes the traditional way of dealing with problems that arise from living. Killing is not with the bayonet or with the bomb only, but also with the attitudes, the opinions, the judgements and the gestures that one uses to destroy others. We are taught to hate from childhood: a parent tells his children, 'Don't see so-and-so, he's not a nice man', or 'She's not one of us', and so the seed of hate is sown. The misery of it all is the importance given to prejudice, to established values and to dangerous things like nationalism and separate gods to which one has become accustomed. The collecting of garbage and the representation of God are specialized functions that people create as monopolies, and so these very people become the source of violence.

Most of us know all these things, some of us intellectually and others with emotional concern, but humanity seems to be unable to start anew, to look at all these problems with fresh eyes. Those who revolt against the past fall into another trap. This has been the historical process: the new gods become the old gods overnight.

Observing all this unemotionally, and certainly not intellectually, we see that action that is not born of ideas but out of quite a different state of mind becomes an urgent necessity. After all, love is not the monopoly of any State or any religion; it cannot be domesticated or tamed and put into the framework of a family. It is fierce and passionate, without the dead ashes of yesterday. Action born of this is relationship and this is the only way out.

65. A DIFFERENT EDUCATION

The essence of culture
is complete harmony

Although the word education has misapplied meanings, it must be used to convey generally what is going on in the world. The use of that word, whether in the East or the West, implies attending classes from childhood through to university, taking degrees and accumulating a great deal of information about various subjects – from theoretical physics to the growing of vegetables, from music to medicine, and so on. This cultivation of memory has become a necessity in the present social and economic structure. To have a good job in the field of education or in the field of politics or in business, a degree is considered essential. To acquire this degree you must conform to the structure of knowledge and to the established order of society or of the State – whether that State be socialist, communist or capitalist. In acquiring these varieties of knowledge, the brain must retain a great deal of facts, experience and tradition. Through the course of many years in acquiring information, and applying it in practice, the brain inevitably must be conditioned and so it becomes mechanical, though it has freedom to function within its limited area. The whole of existence is aimed at the earning of a livelihood, to conform to a pattern and to living with the known.

The exercise of the brain is confined to the field of knowledge, the known. The known is the past, as is knowledge, and from that the future or the present is built. However intricate and subtle knowledge is, it is always within the field of time, the known. And thought has its roots in the past. Thought may go very far, explore many fields into the past or into the future, into abstract science or into anthropology; it may explore space.

From childhood the brain is trained to be competitive, to be ambitious, to worship success, which gives importance to the "me", the self, the ego; and so the essence of cooperation is destroyed. All this is generally what is called education even in the higher forms which give status in society, which has become more important than function. Throughout the world this is what is called education, and therefore one begins to question or doubt that very word.

Culture is something totally different. The word implies not only the cultivation of knowledge, but also the total essence of man, both inner and outer. This division is artificial; complete harmony in which there is no division is the real. The present cultures of the world are fast fading, and because they are disappearing they are being replaced by knowledge and not by wisdom. The essence of culture is complete harmony. This harmony is the very core of the religious mind. Without religion there is no culture; but not the religion of organized propaganda, which all religions are, nor the personal search for some vast experience. The religious mind is not based on any belief, faith or authority; it is the total absence of the self. When, in the disintegration of any culture, sex, gurus and authority with its followers spring up – like mushrooms in a damp field of rotting forest – then tradition and the book become all-important. This is what is happening basically, deep down in the human mind, when fanciful mysticism, pleasing visions, self-projected gods and saviours are pursued. When knowledge, the known, has become of supreme importance, then the mind searches out mysteries, runs after the experiences of others and establishes new gods.

Culture is the door to reality, which is not in philosophies, psychology and analysis. Without the beauty of religion, culture has no meaning. It is like a lovely flower without the perfume, and we tear the flower to pieces to find the perfume.

Love is harmony, which cannot be cultivated, as knowledge can be, so there is a widening gap between the known and the harmony of perception. The seeing is the doing, but knowledge, because of its time quality, prevents instant action. The religious mind has this quality of immediate action.

A different kind of education is necessary. It is not the mere cultivation of memory with all its emphasis on compulsion, conformity, imitation, leading to violence, but the total culture of man in which the "you" and the "me" disappear and are not replaced by the State

197

or by a new figure of sanctity. This different education is concerned with knowledge, with freedom, with what is, and to go beyond what is.

Wisdom is not in any book or in the perfection of knowledge. It is in the movement of freedom in learning. There is no end to learning; and wisdom is the ending of sorrow.

66. FUNDAMENTAL FREEDOM

Without responsibility
there is no freedom

Freedom is one of the most important factors in life. Man has fought politically for freedom all over the world. Religions have promised freedom, not in this world but in another. In the capitalist countries, individual freedom exists to some degree, and in the communist world it has been denied. From ancient times freedom has meant a great deal to man, and there have been its opponents, not only political but religious – through the Inquisition, by excommunication, tortures and banishments, and the total denial of man's search for freedom. There have been wars and counter-wars fought for freedom. This has been the pattern of man's endeavours for freedom throughout history.

Freedom of self-expression and freedom of speech and thought exists in some parts of the world, but in others it does not. Those who have been conditioned revolt against their backgrounds, and react in immature ways. This reaction, which takes different forms, is called "freedom". The reaction to politics is often to shun the field of politics. One economic reaction is to form small communities based on some ideology or under the leadership of some one person, in which authority is denied and an attempt is made to be self-supporting, but these generally disintegrate. The religious reaction against established organizations of belief is to revolt, either by joining other religious organizations or by following some guru or leader or by joining some cult. Or one denies the whole religious endeavour. Don't all these indicate mere outward movements toward freedom?

One thinks of freedom only as freedom of movement, either physical or the movements of thought. It appears one always seeks freedom on the surface, the right to go from here to there, to think what one likes, to do what one likes, to choose, and to seek wider experiences. Surely this is a rather limited freedom, involving a great deal of conflict, wars and violence. Inner freedom is something entirely different. When there is deep, fundamental freedom, which has its roots not in the idea of freedom but in the reality of freedom, then that freedom covers all movement, all the endeavours of man. Without this freedom, life will always be an activity within the limited circle of time and conflict.

So when we talk of freedom we are talking of the fundamental issue. It is not freedom from something, but the quality of a mind and heart that are free, and in which direction does not exist. Freedom from something is only a modified continuity of what has been, and therefore it is not freedom. When there is direction, and therefore choice, freedom cannot exist; for direction is division and hence choice and conflict.

There is no such thing as individual freedom, but only freedom. The word individual in its very meaning implies indivisible, not an entity opposed to the collective. But we have made a concept of individuality with its peculiar characteristics, tendencies, and so on, which are the response of conditioning, and we oppose it to the collective. This conditioning is part of the culture – economic, social, and so on – in which the mind is educated. Freedom lies beyond this conditioning, not within the field of consciousness with the content that makes up consciousness. The responsibility that lies beyond conditioning is different from the responsibility of so-called freedom.

The responsibility of a conditioned mind is irresponsibility, which can be perceived in the present cultures of society, whether of the East or of the West. This irresponsibility is shown in education, in social injustice, in national divisions with different ideologies leading to competition, wars, starvation, affluence and poverty. The irresponsibility of organized religions is shown in their support and maintenance of these cultures. These religions preach morality, but sustain corruption. They are at war with each other, asserting that they alone have the truth, that their gods and saviours are the real. This irresponsibility is shown when an intermediary is placed between the real and the human. This irresponsibility is shown when temples, mosques and churches become a power in the land.

Responsibility has quite a different meaning when there is freedom. Responsibility does not deny freedom: they go together. When there is the deep fundamental reality of freedom, responsibility is concerned with the whole of life and not with one fragment of life; it is concerned with the whole movement and not with some particular movement; it is concerned with the whole activity of the mind and the heart and not with one particular activity or direction. Freedom is the total harmony in which responsibility is as natural as the flower in the field. That response is not induced or imposed; it is the natural outcome of freedom. Without responsibility, there is no freedom. To respond to every challenge out of freedom is responsibility. It is the inadequate response that is irresponsibility. The mind that is dependent in attachment becomes irresponsible to the whole.

So freedom is love, which in its very nature is responsible to the flower by the roadside, and to the neighbour whether the neighbour is next door or a thousand miles away.

Compassion is the very essence of freedom.

67. RELATIONSHIP

Relationship is society

Freedom is not something you set out to find. It isn't a thing to be cultivated. It comes naturally, through the negation of what it is not. It is not a reaction, and this is a basic thing that must be understood. The reaction to what is is a continuation of what is in a different form. It may be modified, it may be structured differently, it may be rationalized and made to function, but this is not freedom. This reaction may take the form of opinion, evaluation, of judgement, but this is not freedom. The reaction to an old order, to tradition, to various forms of authority is not freedom. The reaction of one's particular tendency, idiosyncrasy or characteristics, which are the response of one's conditioning, is not freedom. The reaction to having been told to restrain, to control, to obey by going off in some different direction, pleasant or unpleasant, neurotic or rational, is not freedom. And going from one orthodoxy to another, from one belief to another, from one authority to another, however pleasant, is not freedom; exchanging one ideology for another is in no way freedom. To do what one likes is an imagined freedom. To assert one's own individuality, and the identification of one's desires with something that is romantically or mystically great, is not freedom.

Freedom is the understanding of all this, not only verbally but actually transcending all this. That is why it is so important to observe clearly the repetitive reactions in the guise of freedom and experience. Through negation of these reactions and in transcending them, one is confronted with the actual, the what is. The what is is relationship.

Relationship is society, this society which humanity has put together. As you and I have put this society together, we are responsible for the society. It is our society, not "theirs". It is not created only by your parents, you also are responsible for it. You as a human being are creating this society and you are part of this society. So you are the society, the world.

It is your relationship with another, your behaviour, your conflicts, your ambitions, your competition that has brought about this structure in which we live. Again, this is very important to understand. Understanding is not at the intellectual or verbal level; understanding is action. It is not first understanding and then action afterwards; they are simultaneous, they go together. This relationship is not only with your intimate friend or with your neighbour, but with people you never see, who may be thousands of miles away. The responsibility of relationship is enormous. You cannot live without relationship; life is relationship. However much one may want to isolate oneself for neurotic reasons or for some form of specialization, one is still in relationship.

So relationship is of the highest importance. There is no relationship if your daily activity is centred around your own egotistic activities. There is no relationship if you build a wall around yourself because you have been hurt, or because you cannot have what you want, or because you are trying to fulfil yourself in a particular activity. There is no relationship if you are tethered to a strong belief or a conclusion, either one given by another or one you have put together yourself. There is no relationship if you belong to one group as opposed to another, or if you have committed yourself to one course of action based on some rational or irrational conclusion. There is no relationship if you have an image about yourself or about another. That image may be based on your knowledge, your experience, and these images, either traditional or your own, separate you from another. Where there is separation of any kind, national, religious, economic or social, there must be conflict in yourself and so with the world. Where there is conflict there is no relationship.

Love has no conflict. When love becomes pleasure, there begins conflict. Desire is not love, and in the fulfilment of desire love is denied.

Relationship is not only with human beings, but with nature, with the tree and with the animal. When we lose contact with nature, we lose contact with each other. When you lose contact with the birds, the shy and timid quail, then you lose contact with your child and the person across the street. When you kill an animal to eat, you are also cultivating insensitivity which will kill that man across the border. When you lose contact with the enormous movement of life, you lose all relationship. Then you, the ego with all its fanciful urges, demands and pursuits, become all-important, and the gulf between you and the world widens in endless conflicts.

So relationship and freedom go together. The denial of what is not relationship and the negation of what is not freedom bring about an action of total responsibility. And this is love.

68. AUTHORITY

Freedom has no authority

Freedom brings with it creativity. This has nothing to do with the creation that comes through conflict. There is no freedom if the mind is conditioned. Conditioning is the result of social, economic or religious cultures. When the mind is conditioned, it functions in a very limited specialized area. This functioning, whether it is highly technological or a movement in the field of conditioning, is generally called creativity. This conditioned movement generates its own energy, and this energy is expressed in literature, science, music and the various humanities.

But all this is within the field of conditioning, whether it be narrow or wide. This activity makes a path which is accepted and followed, but again this is still within the confines of conditioning. Man seeks freedom within those limits and the exercise of that freedom is called freedom of will or choice, but it is still directed or shaped by conditioning. It is like a man in prison seeking freedom within its walls, whether narrow or wide. This is not freedom.

Freedom is something totally different. It is the understanding of conditioning both verbally and non-verbally, so that the mind transcends it. This freedom is not in a book or to be found through another, and it is not an ideal. It is not to be purchased through any practice or discipline, for practice and discipline imply sanction and authority. In this freedom there is no direction or authority. This freedom is intelligence and it is responsible. It is not dictated by circumstances or events. This freedom is total negation of the entire structure of the prison which thought has built round itself. This very negation is the positive action of freedom. This freedom cannot exist where there is disorder. It is outer and inner disorder that brings about the necessity of authority, the dictator, the ruler.

Freedom has no authority. It has never known authority. It is not the rejection of authority, but is the non-existence of it. Both authority and law, outer and inner, are put together by thought. The outer authority, sometimes rational, sometimes irrational, has its place and its responsibility; one cannot brush it aside, and the intelligence of freedom knows its limitation and its necessity. The inner authority, which is subtler and deeper, is much more complex. Guidelines, which seem to give certainty and assurance, become a pattern, the norm, which becomes the authority. This authority may be traditional, a person, a symbol or an idea. The mind, being aware consciously or unconsciously of its own disturbance and disorder, brings about both the outer and the inner authority. A disorderly group soon finds its leader who then directs and controls. The reaction to this is not freedom. The understanding of the nature of this disorder and the disturbance and the going beyond them is freedom.

The acceptance of authority is caused by disturbance and disorder. The effect is the authority, and the reaction to that is to conform or to deny. This very denial assumes another form of authority. Where there is no freedom, there must be authority. This brings about suppression, control or escape, and the very movement of these culminates in a principle or belief, a standard which assumes dominance. The cause is never permanent; the cause becomes the effect and the effect becomes the next cause. When this is clearly understood, not intellectually but actually, then the negation of this chain is freedom. Knowledge has its own authority: experience and memory. But as long as one remains within that field, the creative movement of freedom is non-existent. Freedom is space, and space is order.

69. COMPULSION

Learn without compulsion

There is no freedom when there is disorder. Disorder begets authority, and authority in any form is evil – if one can use that word evil. Where there is freedom, disorder or the lack of order cannot exist, yet the disorderly mind is always seeking freedom. Such a mind will define freedom in terms of its own confusion. A disordered mind seeking freedom or asserting freedom has no meaning whatsoever. A disordered mind invites the discipline imposed by authority in different forms – politically, religiously, socially, and so on – political tyranny and religious dogma.

What are we being educated for? Is it to make the mind conform to the patterns set by previous generations, or is it to understand and go beyond the whole structure of our disordered life both outwardly and inwardly? Is it merely to acquire knowledge or is it to free ourselves from disorder and so bring about a new society?

Obviously if one gives serious thought to this, education is to bring about in the mind a total freedom so that it is capable not only of ordering its own life but also, in this very process, of bringing about a different social structure. This is action which [is not that of] the mind that is committed to a particular course of action or a particular belief, ideal or action influenced by the environment.

We are concerned with education and how to bring about order without compulsion. Where there is compulsion in any form, subtle or obvious, there is not only conformity, imitation, but also fear is bred. Our problem in these schools is how to educate without any form of authority and compulsion. Knowing how authority comes into being and the effects of compulsion, how is a disordered mind to free itself from its confusion naturally, without effort? The students come from disordered families and society. They themselves are confused, uncertain. They react from their conditioning. Their revolt, which they call freedom, is the response of their confusion. So that is the state of the students. They want security, affection; this cannot be if there is compulsion. In their anxious revolt they reject not only the word discipline with its authority but also any form of coercion. The more sensitive they are, the stronger are their reactions, and their revolt is unfortunately expressed in many superficial ways.

Education is not the right word, but we have to use it to convey a meaning that implies the real cultivation of the human mind in all its relationships and activities. The cultivation of the mind and the heart is our responsibility.

The student comes already conditioned, and from that conditioning his reactions are his temperament, his peculiarity, his desire to fulfil. So the educator, who is also conditioned with his own peculiarities, in his responsibility of relationship to the student must be aware of his own limitations as well as those of the student; so both are educating themselves together. If the educator is disorderly in his private life, and outwardly assumes an orderly life, his word has no significance. When he tells the student to be orderly, he becomes a hypocrite. So the educator needs education as well as the student. This is the principal action – that both are learning – and so the spirit of authority doesn't enter at all into this relationship. When this is clearly and deeply understood, then one has to establish a relationship in which compulsion and conformity cease altogether.

How is the student, being confused and disorderly, to learn without compulsion to be orderly? Order is necessary. Order is expressed in behaviour. Order is the very nature of the universe. There is order in nature. Only when man interferes in nature is there disorder, because he himself is disorderly. Order is the action of virtue. Order is love. There is no order when there is effort or contradiction. Order is the highest form of intelligence. Intelligence is not intellectual capacity; it is not the opposing of opinions and conclusions; it is not the mere reasoning capacity, however logical that may be. Intelligence is the highest form of sensitivity outwardly and inwardly toward others as well as toward oneself.

How is this intelligence to be awakened? Obviously not through any method or system. It is possible only when both the older and the younger are aware of the world about them, of nature and of their own activities, are aware of the events that are going on in the world and their own inward reactions. This awareness is not a thing to be practised and made mechanical. One becomes aware of the total activities of one's mind and body, the way one sits, stands, walks. One listens to one's voice and the significance of words, one's opinions and attitudes, the language of look and gesture, the language of behaviour and its effect on others. All this implies an awareness of one's own self-centred motives and activities.

We have separated ourselves logically from the world. This separation is linguistic rather than real. The actuality is that we are the world and the world is us. We are not totally aware of this. We may accept this idea intellectually, but it is not an actuality. In the same way, we divide ourselves as the body and the mind, as sentiment or emotion. We never look at ourselves as a whole. This fragmentation is caused by thought, and through thought this awareness is not possible. In this awareness, identification with one's own desires and choice disappear, so both young and old are learning to be. Awareness isn't only in the classroom, but at the table, on the playground. It is to be learnt also when one is walking alone across the fields or sitting quietly in one's room. From this sensitive awareness comes intelligence.

How is this to be conveyed and sustained? Obviously by talking about it, by observing what is happening about one and in one's own reactions. It is this intelligence that will bring order. When this awareness is acting, punctuality, behaviour, politeness, respect, all become a natural thing, not self-imposed or compelled. The teacher and the taught are one. Therefore the observer is the observed. When this relationship is established – and it can only take place when there is the quality of intelligence – there is the possibility of a psychologically different human being.

It is for this that these schools exist, and it is our responsibility to see that this comes into being.

70. DISCIPLINE

Learning is discipline

When you look around you, not so much in the human world as in nature, in the heavens, you see an extraordinary sense of order, balance and harmony. Every tree and flower has its own order, its own beauty; every hilltop and every valley has a sense of its own rhythm and stability. Though man tries to control the rivers and pollutes their waters, they have their own flow, their own far-reaching movement. Apart from man, in the seas, in the air and the vast expanse of the heavens there is an extraordinary sense of purity and orderly existence. Though the fox kills the chicken, and the bigger animals live on the little animals, what appears to be cruelty is a design of order in this universe, except for man. When man doesn't interfere, there is great beauty of balance and harmony. This harmony can exist only in freedom, not in restriction and not in conflict.

Everything in nature has its season, its dying and rebirth. It is only man that lives in confusion, in conflict, in disorder. If you have watched in a wood, all the living things have their instinctual ways, their own pattern of life which is immemorial and endless. But man is shaped by his selfishness, and his so-called spontaneity is within the field of his self-interest. He is shaped and controlled by the culture, the environment in which he lives. Society tells him what to do; the elders try to shape the minds of the young to conform, to obey and to live in a very small space both outwardly and inwardly. Reform is the breaking of one pattern only to conform to another. We live a very short life, in conflict, in fear and sorrow. Only when we are very young do we seem to be utterly happy and unconcerned. All this soon fades, and then begins the weary conflict of existence.

In all this turmoil there is neither freedom nor the order of spontaneity, for freedom is a great sense of spontaneity. In society, in the family, in a school, if there is no order there is no relationship. And yet we want a relationship which is really an attachment to another without an inward sense of harmony, wholeness, integrity. If you walk past a parade ground you see the poor soldier being drilled day after day by the beat of the drum and the voice of the sergeant to obey, to conform and to follow. He is made into a machine to kill and to protect himself. In similar ways from childhood we are drilled to protect ourselves by conforming to the old or to the new. This drilling goes on in the office, in the workshop, in the church, in the school. This is called order, and this is what concerns most parents. This has been going on generation after generation, and the gap between two generations is only an interval in which a new pattern takes shape.

Is it not possible to have order without effort, without the strife between those who see that order is necessary and those who rebel against any form of compulsion? Is there an order without conformity? Is there an action that does not lead to routine and boredom? This is one of the problems in our world of relationship. Every intelligent person, whether old or young, sees that order is necessary: getting up, learning, playing, and so on. If you want to be a good golfer, you must swing the club in a certain way; if you want to be a good swimmer, you must learn the strokes. Learning to be a good golfer or tennis player brings its own natural movement of control. This control is not imposed by anyone but the very movement of the hand and arm, of the body is infinitely orderly and subtle. Each trade has its own discipline, and learning is the discipline.

Discipline is an unfortunate word. In it are implied drill, practice, conformity, subjugation, restraint, and the conflict of indolence. The dictionary meaning of the word discipline is to learn – only to learn and nothing else. If you do not want to learn, then parents, the school, society force you to conform whether you like it or not. However new the society may be, it forces you to fit in. The religious have thrived on this through fear and reward. Either you learn through spontaneous interest or you are driven, compelled to learn. When you are compelled to learn, then your knowledge is mechanical and you use that knowledge mechanically. Then you complain that life has no meaning, and you try to escape through various illusions, through daydreaming or fanciful words. Night-clubs, the weekend recreation, the holidays are the trivia of escape. You have narrowed down your life to the family and the responsibility it brings, to endless work and to the inevitable.

Learning without reward or punishment is quite another matter. If you understand and see this very clearly, when you play football, cricket, or when you are studying a subject, you will find that learning frees the mind rather than shapes it. Knowledge by itself shapes the mind, and so the mind becomes old. The schools and universities are making minds old. They condition conformity, for knowledge has become all-important – not learning but acquiring knowledge. It is an old mind that conforms, not the mind that is always learning. In this learning there is freedom in which knowledge can be used when it is needed. There are encyclopaedias, there are computers, so do not make your mind merely the storehouse of the past. This is order.

Questioner: Do you mean to say that I don't have to acquire knowledge of any subject, that I don't have to study?

Krishnamurti: Not at all. When you put that question, what is behind it? Is it that you don't want to study because it bores you? Or are you asking how to learn, that is, how to pay attention? When you don't want to pay attention, don't pay attention. What is important is to have a mind that has never been shaped in conflict, in wanting and not-wanting to pay attention. In that there is conflict. If you want to look out of the window, look out of the window completely without the conflict of saying you must look at the book. Look out of the window with your eyes, your ears, your mind and heart. Then when you look at the book in front of you, whatever the subject may be, look at it in the same way that you looked out of the window. You will, if you have no conflict. This is the primary thing to learn: never under any circumstances to have a conflict. Because you have learnt to look out of the window freely, without any restraint or compulsion, you will look at the book in the same manner, because this is learning. Both are learning: looking out of the window and looking at the book. Learning to be free from conflict is not indifference or allowing yourself to do nothing.

Q: If I get rid of conflict I will then do just what I enjoy.

K: Can you really do what you want? Isn't what you want a reaction to what you have been told to do? Is what you want free of the structure of the society in which you live? What you want is the pursuit of your particular pleasure. Then you will develop a double standard of life. Secretly you will pursue pleasure and openly you will be forced by the culture in which you live to conform to the respectable. So you are developing conflict, wanting your pleasures and not being able to have them, or having them and paying for it. All this obviously maintains conflict. Learning about conflict is the understanding of this whole pattern of the behaviour of pleasure.

Q: Are you denying me pleasure?

K: On the contrary. If I were to deny you pleasure, you would fight, you would become violent. You would find a means to fulfil your pleasure, and so again you would be caught in conflict. We are always caught between punishment and reward, which is fear; to learn about it is freedom from conflict.

Q: Are you saying that discipline is wrong?

K: No, we are not saying that.

Q: Then why do we have rules?

K: Have you listened to what has been said about this question of discipline? Or have you listened only to the part that pleases you? If you have only half-listened, you have drawn a conclusion or an idea, and from that you are going to act or not act according to what pleasure dictates. We said that order is necessary. The whole universe functions in order except man. Man has allowed himself to live in this contradictory condition and from this arises all his misery. Do look at it all in a different way, not in terms of pleasure and punishment, but seeing a way of living in which every form of conflict comes to an end. You have to learn about this and the very learning creates its own order.

71. SANITY

Freedom is sane living in daily life

Freedom is a word that is so loosely used that it no longer has real significance. Though we talk about it endlessly in school, in college, politically and religiously, we really don't want freedom. What we want is complete security in all our ways of life. We revolt against authority but we are really rebelling to express our demand for identity and action. Freedom is really a dangerous thing. It is freedom from the total misery, confusion that exists both inwardly and outwardly. The total denial of the structure of ideas and action based on those ideas is freedom. It is not an expression of rampant individual selfishness. The denial of that too, not verbally but actually, is freedom. To stand alone without isolating oneself is sanity. Sanity means health, wholeness and also holiness. In this state there is no imbalance. This is freedom.

This freedom is not an idea, a concept, but is sane living in our daily life. The action of the insane is one thing but this action is another, leading to the flowering of goodness. If you observe the world about you, you see how insane it all is: mothers sending their sons to war to kill and be killed; the divisions of religion and governments with their conflict and their corruption; the talk of peace while preparing for war; the endless breaking-up of human beings into categories, temperaments, with their gurus and analysts. This insanity has its own activity, which is contradictory, imitative and divisive. Education as it now exists is to conform to the pattern of insanity. This action of the "me" and the "you" is the root of corruption whether it is in the name of society, nation or God. Education is to wean away the mind from this insanity and its activities.

So what is the action of sanity? For we are concerned in life with action: life is action in relationship. There is no your action and my action. If there is, it is insanity operating in us. Man has divided action into a great many varieties, into the categories of a mind that is in itself fragmented.

So there is only action, not the activity of the artist, the writer, the politician, and so on. When action is broken up into man-invented categories, corruption sets in. If this is understood very clearly – that is, when you see the inward truth of this, the fact of this – then action is the outcome of the whole. Then you are not committed to a particular course of action but you are committed to the whole of life, which is action. When you are committed to one particular action that may give you gratification and self-expression, then you will find that that act will lead to self-contradiction and therefore to the wasting of energy. The summation of action is in itself not contradictory and therefore releases great energy. So action is total inaction.

Again one must point out that these are not words, ideas and speculative abstractions but facts. The action of the fact, or what is, is vastly different from the action of an idea. For most people the idea is vastly more important than action: concept and action are two different things; there is space between the two, and in this space is time and the division of action, for action is trying to adjust itself to the idea or conform to the concept or formula, and hence there is conflict. Conflict is this division between idea and action.

Where there is sanity there is action and not the idea of action. We have cultivated the intellect, and so intellect has become tremendously important – the intellect that conceives, formulates, remembers, calculates, imagines. When this operates, there is always regret or forgiveness and dependency on cause-effect. In this, action which has a cause becomes the effect of an earlier cause, a cause which has a motive, which becomes the cause of another action.

Where there is sanity, action has no future. There is no 'I will do' or 'I will try'. There is only the doing which has no time, which has no tomorrow. For love there is no tomorrow. The tomorrow exists only in an action that is based on an idea, and to bridge the action to the concept you need time. So for such an action there is always tomorrow with all its regrets, frustrations and incompleteness.

So you begin to see what action is, not according to somebody who then becomes the authority to be followed. When you yourself see the truth of this wholeness, action has quite a different meaning. The tomorrow altogether disappears, but yet tomorrow exists in your arrangements, the planning of daily life; but this planning is contained in the wholeness and is not separate from it.

There is the action of thought and the action of non-thought. The action of thought has its place, but it does not bring about the flowering of goodness. The action of non-thought does. Thought does not breed love; it breeds satisfaction, pleasure, the self-centred activity which has nothing whatsoever to do with love and goodness. The wholeness of action is love.

Questioner: Are you saying that we must not conform to what other people are doing? It is fun to do what others do; it gives me a sense of companionship. It makes it easier to talk, and also it is fun to get into some trouble. Shouldn't we see what it is like to get into a bit of trouble? Most people do. Won't we learn something from it?

Krishnamurti: Education is to make you sensitive not only to your own particular desires, fancies and troubles but also to those of others. Can you be sensitive – that is, highly intelligent – if you are conforming, if you are copying, however pleasant it may be for the time being, what everybody else does? Will intelligence allow you to get into trouble, and what is there to learn from trouble? You may steal something in a shop or from your friend. If you do you will end up in a police station. Is this the action of sensitivity, intelligence? What do you learn from troubles? Either you learn never to get involved in them or you get excitement, sensation, and you move then from one excitement to another, ever demanding greater sensations. And what do you learn from that?

Do you learn the implications of companionship, that you need to depend on others for your sense of self-esteem, to cover up your insufficiency, your feeling of being wanted in one place but not in another? Do you really learn this or do you merely use the word learning to cover up your demand for excitement? One must have fun, one must be able to laugh and to talk to another, but it must come from inside you. That is youth. To have to go outside yourself to seek fun leads to all kinds of trouble, and that is part of this insanity of the world in which we live. It is like going to a temple or to a church to find God. You may not go there, but you want your little excitement out there somewhere. They are both the same. If you are really learning, it is here and not out there.

Q: I'm not sure that I am clever enough to understand all you have said. I can't refute it or agree with it, but the seriousness with which you say this affects me somewhere. But I feel that is not enough. How does my mind become sharp enough for all this?

K: It is not a matter of being clever at all. That is a horrible word. In it is a great deal of cunning, slight deception, a tinge of hypocrisy, a put-on behaviour. You don't need a clever mind. What you really need, if I may point out, is the capacity to observe, to listen; to observe without all the clamour that lies behind the observation, the noise of opinions, rationalization, condemnation. You can observe very simply a leaf in the breeze; you can observe a fly in the room; and also you can observe your behaviour, why you do this and that, why you are hurt, why you store up the hurt, why you yield and why you are obstinate. Just to observe and to listen without any muttering of your own like and dislike.

You know, to do this you have to pay attention, and the learning of this is attention. And in this is a great deal of fun, much more than you realize. It is fun that comes of itself and that is real. The other kind fades away.

72. ORDER AND FREEDOM

Order is the action of the new,
which is intelligence

Freedom is absolute order: neither freedom nor order is relative. Either you are free or you are not. Either there is complete order in you or there is disorder. Order is harmony. Human beings seem to like to live in disorder both outwardly and inwardly. You see this politically. All governments are corrupt; some more, some less. They are run by people who in themselves are disorderly, ambitious, deceitful, with personal antagonisms and vanities. So there is economic war, the very rich and the very poor and all the miseries that come from the struggles of poverty.

You see this confusion in education, which is mainly concerned with the cultivation of memory as knowledge, disregarding the entire psychological structure of man. You see the expression of this disorder where one group of people are killing another group, preparing for war while talking of peace. Science has become the tool of government. Business and progress are destroying the earth, polluting the air and the waters of the seas.

So outwardly, when you look around, there is chaos, confusion and great misery. And inwardly too, human beings are unhappy, live contradictory lives, struggling endlessly, in conflict, seeking security and not finding it either in belief or in the things they possess. There is sorrow in life and in death. Man's inward disorder brings about the outward structure of disorder. These are all obvious facts. Though we talk about freedom, apparently very few seem to come upon it.

Education is primarily to bring about order in our daily living and in understanding the whole meaning of life. To understand order and live in that order needs the highest form of intelligence, but we are not being educated for this. We are chiefly concerned with the acquisition of knowledge as a means of survival, a conflicting survival in a chaotic world.

Order is an extraordinary thing. It has its own beauty, its own vitality not dependent on environment. You cannot say to yourself that you will be orderly in your ways, your actions and in your thoughts. If you do, you soon find that it creates a pattern of behaviour which then becomes mechanical. This mechanical habit either in thought or in action – and so in behaviour – is part of this confusion. Order is vastly pliable, subtle and swift. You cannot put it in a frame and endeavour to live according to it. Imitation itself is one of the reasons for confusion and conflict. You cannot lay down rules for the movement of order. If you do, then those very rules become the authority which demands obedience and conformity. This again has brought about man's misery.

Then there is the person who must have everything around him just so, with nothing out of place. To him order is everything being in a straight line, and he is neurotically annoyed if that line is twisted or pushed aside. Such a person lives in a cage of his own neurosis. There are various monks and ascetics of the world who have trained their minds and their bodies to obey; their God can be approached only through the doors of strict belief and acceptance. Discipline is the drill of habit in the name of virtue, in the name of the State, in the name of God, peace, or what you will.

So you see this all around you every day of your life. In this you are caught, you are part of it. You may deny discipline, order, and cling to an idea of what you think is freedom, but your very concept is a denial of freedom. Freedom is not a concept, an idea, but a reality. It is non-verbal, not put together by thought as a reaction. The total negation of the disorder in which one lives is freedom.

So what is order? The definition according to the dictionary is one thing, and according to your own personal reasoning, inclination or temperament is another. We are concerned with the meaning of that word in the dictionary and not what you think it is. We are concerned with it objectively and not from any personal reaction. The personal point of view about anything distorts what is. The fact is important, not what you think about what is. When you look at the whole movement of life from a personal, conditioned reaction or opinion, then you break up life into the "me" and the "you"; the "you" is the outer, the "me" is the inner, and so conflict begins. This fragmentation is the main cause of inward and outward confusion and conflict. Order comes about in a mind that is not fragmented or broken up by thought.

The order of thought is one thing, and the order of a mind that is whole is another. One leads to mischief, and the other leads to the flowering of goodness. The order of thought as law has its place, but the order of thought in conduct and relationship becomes disorder, for thought is the activity of fragmentation. Thought has divided people as nations, as sectarian religions, as "we" and "they", as communist and non-communist. There is no thought without the word, the image, the symbol. This has divided people. Thought has built this monstrous world, and through thought we are trying to create a new world without realizing that thought itself brings about the activities of confusion, division and conflict.

The order of a mind that is whole is something entirely different, and here comes the difficulty. When you read this statement, you are translating it into a thought process, and so the reading of it is an abstraction. Having made an abstraction of the statement, you then try to match it with an existing abstraction in your memory. When there is no match, you say you do not understand what the statement means. You say you understand when they conform. So be aware of what is happening in your mind, how quickly thought intervenes, that you never listen or read with a mind that is not burdened with the past. Knowledge is the past. This knowledge has its utilitarian meaning, but when that knowledge is used in our relationships then confusion, conflict and sorrow begin.

So order is the action of the new, which is intelligence.

Now let us go back and look at all this. We were saying that absolute order is freedom. This absolute order can exist only when conflict of every kind has come to an end in you. When there is this order, then you will not ask about the disorders in the world. You will ask that question only when you are the world and the world is you. When you are not of the world, which means there is absolute order in you, then your relation to the world has undergone a total change. You are in the world but not of it.

So become aware of the disorder of the world and the disorder in you. Then there is no division between you and the world, there is only disorder. When the mind is choicelessly aware of this disorder without any movement of thought, then order comes unbidden. What you invite is not order: your invitation comes out of disorder. Order and disorder are not related, they are not opposites. Order does not come about through the conflict of the opposites. Either there is order or there is not. Any pretence at orderliness is born of disorder.

Where there is order there is humility.

EDITORS NOTE

This new collection of J Krishnamurti's Letters to the Schools combines the letters originally published in Volume I (1981) and Volume II (1985) with seventeen previously unpublished letters from earlier years. The letters from Volume I, numbered 1 to 37 in this edition, were dated fortnightly between 1st September 1978 and 1st March 1980. The letters from Volume II, numbered from 38 to 55, were dated as follows: four monthly in November and December 1981 and January and February 1982, ten fortnightly from 1st October 1982 to 15th February 1983, and four fortnightly in October and November 1983.

The new letters included are numbered 56 to 72, and were dated between January and May 1968 (numbers 56 to 64) and fortnightly between 1st March and 1st July 1973 (numbers 65 to 72). These additional letters, although written earlier, are placed at the end.

The letters were originally dictated to a secretary, who typed them and sent mimeographed copies to each school.

Thanks to Mr K Krishnamurthy for valuable detailed editing suggestions.

Ray McCoy

www.ingramcontent.com/pod-product-compliance
Lightning Source LLC
LaVergne TN
LVHW041153080426
835511LV00006B/578